CRAZY FAITH

When Jesus Guides the Journey

Garry Bishop

CRAZY FAITH – When Jesus Guides the Journey

This book is a true work of nonfiction. Some names may have been changed to protect those still on the mission field.

Author Contact: crazyfaithbook@gmail.com

Scripture References:

Cover design and layout by Leonard Buscemi

All photos by Garry Bishop

ISBN: 979-8-218-37637-6

Dedication

This book is dedicated to four true heroes of the faith who gave me encouragement and fellowship while in Afghanistan.

They will always remain in my heart as cherished friends and faithful martyrs. Werner Groenewald and his children Jean-Pierre and Rodé, who gave their lives when terrorists attacked their home while they were serving Jesus in Afghanistan, and dear Hannelie, wife and mother who lost her entire family in that attack.

Acknowledgements

I especially want to thank my beautiful wife Janet, for having the grace to put up with Crazy Garry for so many years, and for helping with the final editing and formatting of this book.

I would also like to thank Troy Zinszer and Troy Tyler for lending their talents, advice, and suggestions so that my experiences with Jesus could be better expressed. And a special thank you to Noelle Howe who was an answer to prayer by helping me with the initial editing.

Prologue

The monarch butterflies were migrating to Mexico and a swarm of them stopped in my yard to visit the flowers. While walking through the garden one day, my mind immersed in a myriad of questions, I bent down to study one of the butterflies in detail. In my mind it was as though I could see the butterfly on a molecular level. I could see that this tiny creature was designed and made with amazingly intricate detail, details which only provided elegance and beauty but were not needed for its survival.

It was then that I realized how involved God is in creating and giving life in an amazingly beautiful way to something as simple and seemingly insignificant as a butterfly. I was so moved that I cried out loud, "God, you are involved in the minutest details of your creations! How much are you involved in my own life that I don't understand?"

Overwhelmed by the greatness and wonder of God, the Creator, I felt at that moment that something was about to change.

Introduction

This book will relate some, but certainly not all, of the many amazing events experienced on the mission field where I witnessed Jesus operating in miraculous and wonderful ways. Those encounters have allowed me to grow in faith and to realize extraordinary faith, or as I have learned to call it, Crazy Faith.

In a sense my life has been a prolonged battle between satan trying to end my life and Jesus keeping me alive. When Jesus called me to serve Him by sharing the gospel of salvation with lost souls, I went wherever He asked me to go and did whatever He asked me to do, no matter how crazy it seemed at the time. Because I am resolved to put my faith wholly in Him, I have often seen the hand of God operating in incredible ways, sometimes supernatural and unexplainable in human terms. After experiencing those supernatural events I can now believe Jesus for everything. *Jesus said to him, "If you can believe, all things are possible to him who believes."* [Mark 9:23]. Nothing provides me more joy and peace than seeing things happen that only God can do. And since Jesus commissioned me to write this book, I trust you will be sharing my joy as you share in my experiences.

Some of my greatest heroes are mentioned in Hebrews Chapter 11, such as the ones who were burned at the stake or sawn in half for their faith. Unimaginable pain and violence are described, yet men and women of Christ have willingly endured such things. They have calmly surrendered to such violence against them, rather than deny the One who saved them. Those are my heroes, the unnamed who possessed such extraordinary faith.

There are many ways that Jesus will protect us when we obey His command to *"Go into all the world and preach the gospel to every creature."* [Mark 16:15]. The fact that some places I am called to are extremely dangerous does not concern me. I am serving under the orders of the Creator of the world and all that exists, the King of kings and the Lord of lords. Also, I have the examples of eleven of the closest disciples of Jesus, ten of whom were martyred because of their obedience. I know for certain that if I am obeying Jesus' instructions as confirmed in His Word, that I will be under the protection of Jesus and His angels. I know that nothing can harm me unless Jesus allows it. I also know that He will only allow things to happen to me that are ultimately good for His Kingdom and that are according to His will. If my obedience to His Word results in my death, then I will still be thankful as I am ushered into His presence in heaven.

When Jesus walked the earth in His human body, the New Testament records that His attention was most attracted when men and women expressed extraordinary (crazy) faith in Him. Crazy faith that defies human reason draws Jesus. Crazy faith that holds tightly to an expectation that the Creator of the universe is personally involved and will intervene in their situation. An expectation of the supernatural regardless of the form it might take. Even if their crazy faith meant dying immediately, they considered only what a glorious death it would be, dying for the very One who died for them. Heaven would be abuzz with talk of such great faith. And in the instant of *"...mortality being swallowed up by life."* [2Cor. 5:4], they would be transformed into His presence forever. And if exercising crazy faith meant that Jesus supernaturally rescued them, then their continued life in their human body on earth would have a new and fuller dimension, and a fuller and richer testimony and witness. Crazy faith in Jesus brings the freedom to accept that *no matter what happens to me Jesus is in control. And what happens next, regardless of the trials or pain that it may cause me, will work out for good.* One evening in

Afghanistan I was inspired with another definition for crazy faith: Crazy Faith = reckless abandonment to the will and protection of God.

Contents

Chapter 1

Kabul, Afghanistan

September 18, 2011, was to become a monumental day for me. It was during my fifth trip to Afghanistan since Jesus first sent me to Kabul in 2003. And I had talked my way into a meeting with the senior mullah at the largest Shia Mosque in Kabul.

We exchanged greetings and I was introduced to his security detail and assistants accompanying him. The mullah asked me what I would like to discuss. I told him that I had been reading the Qur'an and I had found some interesting things that I wanted to discuss with him. I pointed out some of the positive things that the Qur'an said about Jesus and noted that more than fifty times the Qur'an refers to the Bible. After further discussion I asked him why the Muslims I've met in Afghanistan did not read the Bible, as the Qur'an instructs them to do. I told him that Muslims whom I've asked this question said that their mullahs and elders warned them against reading the Bible because the Qur'an had replaced it. I asked the Mullah if it was true that the mullahs and elders were teaching such things. His reply was, "Of course we know that the Bible of today has been changed and corrupted."

Before the meeting I had determined to control my emotions, but that determination was now lost and instead the Holy Spirit took over. It was like something was being forced up from my belly and out of my mouth and I literally roared, "*NO!*" I continued passionately, "How can you say such a thing? You call yourself a religious leader of your people, and yet you dishonor and disrespect the Word of God by saying the Bible has been changed and corrupted. You must know that the Qur'an says that God is all powerful and that nobody can change His Word. And here you are saying that man has changed and corrupted the Bible, which even the Qur'an says is the true Word of God. That is blasphemy!"

I glanced over at the other men in the room and their mouths were hanging open with a look of frozen fear. None of them uttered a word. The mullah appeared to be in shock and stared at me with a look of disbelief. He quickly regained his composure and announced, "I have a meeting to get to. Can you come back on Tuesday at one o'clock and we can resume our discussion?" I suspected that by inviting me back he almost certainly had something nefarious that he was planning for me. Yet I wanted to return to share the gospel with him and ask him to repent and trust Jesus for his salvation.

The rest of this encounter was truly miraculous because when I returned to meet with the mullah, Jesus supernaturally kept me from being harmed or killed. I am still amazed as I recall the details. But before I share the conclusion of this story, I want to share the journey that led up to this point so you can better understand how I came to be in this most unusual and dangerous situation.

Chapter 2

A Difficult Youth

My dad was totally opposed to God, especially Jesus. He taught us that there was no God and that religion, especially Christianity, was nothing but BS. He was a staunch, uncompromising atheist. Later in life my dad softened his stance on atheism a bit and he became instead a self-proclaimed agnostic. An agnostic to dad was someone who doesn't know and doesn't care. It was in this environment of unbelief in God that I grew up.

When I was 14 my dad and his business partner pursued a land development opportunity in a remote and underdeveloped mountainous wilderness in Canada called Alta Lake. Years later this area became known as Whistler Mountain, a famous ski resort. Our new community had few people when we arrived, although the population doubled or tripled during the summer months. We were forty miles from the nearest grocery store and my high school. My two older brothers soon moved away for college and work, leaving my younger sister and me at home. I didn't have any friends my age who lived in the area and I was terribly lonely.

The absence of friends and my brothers formed me into a social hermit. Having a lot of time on my hands I spent most of that time thinking. During my mid-teens much of my thinking was focused on seeking answers to life's greatest questions: "What is the meaning of life?" "What are we on this earth for?" "Is there a God?"

The small town where I spent my last two years of high school was backwards in many respects. The First Nation people lived on a reservation outside of town, and many of the residents of the town were very bigoted against them. I didn't fit in with that mindset since my mom taught me early in life not to be prejudiced against anyone. I should mention that I was the only long-haired, pot smoking hippy attending school in this highly bigoted community. I was so socially isolated that school became intolerable. Unfortunately, my home life wasn't any better.

My dad was a good man, but his struggling business created significant stress which led to heavy drinking. Dad was drunk most nights, and I became the target for almost continual mental and emotional abuse. Eventually I ended up in the middle of a full-blown breakdown. I was unable to focus on anything productive and I was continually suicidal.

I was intelligent enough, so my grades remained excellent, but I reached a point where I was too stressed from my miserable and isolated environment to continue participation in school. I quit school just three months before graduation. My dad had always made it very clear that if I quit school I would have to leave home. So, I needed to leave home, but I had very little money and nowhere to go.

A Cabin in the Woods

I struggled to figure out where I could live. The only real option I had was a long-abandoned mining camp in the woods a couple of miles from our house. It was hidden deep in the forest with a partially overgrown narrow dirt road. I stumbled upon it on one of my walks. All the old cabins had long ago crumbled under the weight of heavy winter snow, except for one. It was a single room cabin with all the walls still standing and a partially collapsed roof. I decided to fix it up and live there. I scavenged wood from the other collapsed cabins and with the little money I had saved, bought tar paper, a cheap wood stove and some stovepipe, a kerosene lamp, a small propane camping stove, and some cheap foam rubber for a mattress. There was no electricity, so I used the kerosene lamp for light. No running water either, so I bathed in and got my drinking water from a glacier-fed creek about four hundred yards from the cabin.

I lived in that cabin for over a year. Without disturbances and without conveniences it is still the most peaceful place I have ever lived. That summer I planted trees with a reforestation contractor, and I made enough money in a couple months to last me for the rest of my time in the cabin.

The following spring the government Forestry Department discovered my cabin, which was on government land. I was given 14 days to vacate. I spoke with the head of the Forestry Department, but he wouldn't listen to my reasoning of why my living there was a benefit to the forest, and eventually they burned my cabin to the ground.

Christians

Something very significant and life changing happened while I was living in the cabin. A couple of years earlier, while still living at home, I met a girl who became my girlfriend. She was the daughter of a building contractor who had come from Vancouver to Alta Lake for the summer to build a cabin for a couple who had bought a buildable lot from my dad.

My girlfriend, her older sister, and I spent a lot of time together that summer. I knew that her family were all Christians, although I didn't understand what a Christian was at that point. Since my dad had said it was all BS, for a long time I didn't ask her about what she believed, nor did she offer any information. One day she and her sister were at our house listening to music and I put on a song that spoke about religion and heaven. Suddenly they both looked at each other and walked out of the room without saying anything. When they came back in, I asked them why they had left the room. They said that because of their beliefs they had a problem with the words of the song. When I asked what the problem was, and what they believed, they were unwilling to talk to me about it. The more I asked them to tell me about what they believed, the angrier they became with me. So, I dropped it.

In my search for the answers to life I had done a personal study on world religions when I was in high school. Naturally due to my dad's influence I had a negative attitude about Christians. Also my girlfriend's Christian parents would not allow me in their home because I was not a Christian, so I excluded Christianity from my studies. I had been taught there was no God, yet I always felt that there must be something more to life. What I was experiencing in life was neither satisfying nor fulfilling. In fact, life was horribly hurtful and depressing, and seemingly not worth living. For some reason even at the early age of 14 I had a deep conviction of my own personal sin. I reasoned with myself that if there was a God and a heaven, I could not possibly be good enough to win His approval and go to heaven. I felt like I was a lost soul and was deeply depressed and suicidal. I continued to search for the truth. What else could I do?

Searching still for the answers to life and finding nothing helpful in religion, I turned to psychedelic drugs. I was seeking a spiritual experience that would reveal God to me. At times when I was under the influence of drugs, I would feel close to the truth that I was seeking. But when the effect of the drugs wore off, I was right back to a confused and depressed state. Each religion I studied had some interesting points, but it seemed that they were all about works. I figured that being such a sinner, I could never do enough good works to outweigh my sinful thoughts and actions. What was the point? There I was, with a lot of knowledge about many world religions, no knowledge at all about what it meant to be a Christian, but with a huge thirst to find out more about God.

Chapter 3

My Day of Salvation

I was visiting my girlfriend in Vancouver when she and her sister had plans to attend an evening Christian meeting in a college auditorium. I asked if I could go with them, and although surprised at my request she agreed. *I had absolutely no idea what was going on.* They were singing songs and praying and praising God. It was like nothing I had ever seen or heard before. I was so confused. I thought Christian meetings were supposed to be stuffy and dull. Yet here were a bunch of young people who just seemed to be in love with Jesus. It didn't seem like they were very organized, and I was surprised by the relaxed atmosphere. I don't think there was even a sermon that evening. If there was, I don't remember it. With no religious upbringing it all seemed very strange and foreign to me. What I didn't know at the time is that Canada and the USA were right smack in the middle of the "Jesus Revolution" aka the "Jesus Movement" of the 1970's. This was not a normal Christian service!

My girlfriend lived more than 80 miles away from my cabin. The church meeting ended late, too late to hitchhike home, so the boyfriend of my girlfriend's sister offered to drive me home. He was a year younger than me. I knew he was a Christian and it was a two-hour drive to my cabin, so I thought, what the heck, we could discuss Christianity! I asked him to tell me about Jesus: who He was, what He did, and what he believed that made him a Christian. He hemmed and hawed, and finally said, "I really don't know that much about Jesus." I asked, "What do you mean? You're a

Christian, aren't you? Just tell me who Jesus was, what He did, and why you believe what you do." He sounded embarrassed when he said, "I was born a Christian. I don't know that much about Jesus. The only thing I really know is that you have to ask Him into your heart." I replied, "That's not helpful. I want to know who He was and what He did."

I was very frustrated, and we sat in silence for a while. Finally, thinking there was nothing to lose I said a silent prayer. It was the first time in my life that I had prayed except for the nursery rhyme prayer most kids were taught to say before they got into bed: *Now I lay me down to sleep...* Desperately I cried out, "God I don't know who You are, and I don't believe in You. Jesus, I don't know the first thing about You, so I can't believe in You. But if You are there, I really need You badly."

Apparently, that is exactly what Jesus had waited to hear me say, and my years of searching were answered rather shockingly. As soon as I finished that silent prayer, I heard a sound that started softly from a distance above me. It sounded like a far-off train or wind just starting to pick up. The sound seemed to be coming from outside the car. At the same time, I saw a light far off in the dark night sky that looked like it was moving towards me. As I watched the light getting larger and brighter, the sound was also increasing. It built up to the point where it sounded like a locomotive or a very strong wind. The light kept advancing and the sound kept increasing until the level was overwhelming. Then the light slammed right into my chest and the sound exploded in my brain. It was like my head and body were exploding from the inside out. I started to laugh and weep at the same time. My friend looked at me in shock asking, "What's going on?" I looked at him and I said, "You don't know who Jesus is? Jesus is the Son of God, who came to the earth and lived a sinless life. Then evil men nailed Him to a cross where He died. Then they put Him in a grave and three days later He was raised from the dead. He died and was raised from the dead so that all our sins could be forgiven."

I didn't know where those words came from; I had never heard them before that I could recall. But I said them with conviction, and I believed it, though I didn't understand at the time what had happened to me. I felt like I was in heaven and was filled with a peace that I had never felt before. It was the peace I had been seeking for so long through drugs and studying world religions. I felt like I could not contain this knowledge in my body and mind. I was filled with exhilaration and praise for God. I didn't understand what had happened, nor did my friend. We spent the rest of the trip in silence, me with a huge grin on my face and an unexplainable longed-for peace in my heart.

Although I knew nothing about Jesus or salvation before that experience, immediately afterward I knew who Jesus was and what He accomplished on the cross. I knew that His death and resurrection had saved me from the punishment for my sins. It wasn't head knowledge, it was a deeper knowledge that permeated my entire being and found a permanent place in me. I had fulfilled the scripture where Jesus said: *"Ask, and it will be given to you; seek, and you will find; knock, and it will be opened to you."* [Matthew 7:7]. The truth of Jesus, the knowledge of who He is and what He did on the cross, has never left me no matter how tough life got, or even when I strayed from following Him. Nor since that day has there been any room in me for doubt that Jesus is my Savior.

I understand that my salvation was dramatic, more so than that of many others. It would break my heart if someone doubted their own salvation experience because they didn't experience something as spectacular as what I experienced in that car. Trust your own experience. God knows what each person needs to draw near to Him.

Most people that become Christians are first introduced to an understanding about Jesus and the message of salvation from another Christian. Unfortunately, no one had attempted to explain the message of salvation to me. Even my friend in the car had not been able to explain salvation.

Since Jesus knows all things, I'm sure He knew that no one in my lifetime would ever try to share the gospel with me. Even at my current age of 69 years old nobody has ever approached me to share the gospel with me, or even handed me a tract. So, I assume Jesus saw no other way to give me the opportunity to accept and receive Him than to respond supernaturally to my feeble attempt at prayer in that car. Maybe He saw that as the *only* opportunity to save me, and He did it in such a spectacular way because I wanted to know the truth so sincerely and desperately.

I told my girlfriend what had happened to me, fully expecting that her and her family would rejoice with me and finally invite me into their home. I was neither invited nor accepted. I assumed that they probably felt this long-haired hippy was beyond the grace of God. I'm sure they could not understand how someone like me could be saved, so they could not believe what happened to me. Maybe they suspected I invented the experience to earn approval for my relationship with their daughter.

So perhaps it was out of curiosity that sometime later her parents finally invited me to their church. I had no idea what was going on at the church, nor did I understand what was expected of me, so I was very uncomfortable. The service seemed like what I had always expected a church service to be, stuffy and dull. I could tell that the other people at the service were uncomfortable with me being there, as I was the only long-haired hippy in the service. I was dressed in tattered blue jeans and a T-shirt, and everyone else was very conservative in their best Sunday clothes. After the church service I was invited into their home for the first (and last) time. They grilled me with questions that I could not answer correctly. I didn't have a Bible, and I had no religious upbringing or experience except my dramatic salvation. I knew nothing about Christianity except the basic gospel that had been supernaturally revealed to me in the car.

For a long while I thought that my salvation experience was all there was. I assumed I would just go on living my life as I did before, only now I was saved. So that's what I did. I didn't have a Bible to read or the understanding to seek one out. I didn't know any Christians other than my girlfriend and her family, and none of them said anything more about Jesus to me during the next two years of our relationship.

I had several near-death experiences when I was young. Looking back now I can see that Jesus alone was keeping me alive, sometimes miraculously. At times I couldn't understand why He didn't just let me die. In hindsight I realize He had a plan for my life even when my bad decisions and behaviors were blinding me to His will. Through it all He was patiently waiting for me to arrive at a point where I would turn to Him for direction and find that there was indeed a plan and a purpose for my life.

Chapter 4

Finding Pastor Bob

It was about four years after I had been saved that I went into a church for only the second time in my adult life. My former girlfriend had mentioned visiting a church in Vancouver named St. Margaret's. It was near where I lived at that time, so I showed up at the church one Sunday morning. The pastor of the church was an old man, Pastor Bob. The sign inside the door read, *Reformed Episcopal Church*. I had no idea what that meant, nor did I care. And at that stage of his ministry, nor did Pastor Bob. After we became friends, Pastor Bob shared his story.

Until the Jesus Revolution hit his church Pastor Bob had worn the traditional robes and neck collar of the denomination. Suddenly there were hippies descending upon his church. Nobody asked them to come, they just showed up. They were unconventional with most of the men sporting long hair, some were malodorous in varying degrees, and many were barefooted. For an established conservative church this was very disconcerting and an imposition upon comfortable routines and traditions.

Here were unchurched and unsophisticated hippies filling the pews next to mostly older, staunch, well-dressed Episcopalians. Pastor Bob struggled with what to do. For a time, he fought against what was happening to his church. Some of the long-term members left the church and the pastor struggled to find an acceptable way to get the hippies to go away. However, Jesus had a better plan and told Pastor Bob to accept everyone who came through the doors, to embrace them, and to teach them about

Him. And that's exactly what he did. In the process, he ditched the religious garb and Jesus baptized him in the Holy Spirit.

Pastor Bob's experiences had prepared him for me, a 21-year-old unchurched, undiscipled, undisciplined, rebellious, drug tripping hippy. My experience with Christianity was confused and distorted. The few Christians I knew rejected me. Yet Jesus had supernaturally and radically saved me. The pastor was a wonderful example of obedience to Jesus, and he welcomed and encouraged me. Pastor Bob was kind and respectful and has been one of the greatest encouragers in my life. For about four months I attended his church each Sunday. I also attended a weekly Bible study one evening a week at his house, and I was baptized in obedience to the Word of God.

I learned much about Jesus from Pastor Bob by being a part of that church community and by participating in the Bible study group. Many young people were on fire for Jesus, reading His Word and worshipping in the Spirit, and the pastor and other leaders allowed the Holy Spirit to have control over the gatherings. The congregation's Sunday services did not follow a tight schedule and there was always freedom for the Holy Spirit to have His way. Everyone was friendly and loving, and it was a wonderful time of friendship and fellowship and learning about Jesus.

It was during this time that I fell in love with the Word of God. I couldn't get enough of it. It had all the answers to life that I had been seeking. It gave me great peace and joy as I learned more about Jesus and what He had said and done. The words of Jesus were like a healing balm to my broken mind and spirit. I bought multiple boxes of New Testaments from the local Bible Society, and I would hand them out to people everywhere I went. I told my parents and all my friends and relatives about Jesus, sharing His message of salvation wherever I went. Though not always received with an open mind, I was not dissuaded.

Chapter 5

Off to Guatemala: A Journey of Obedience

It was early February in 1976 and I was 21 years old, living in Vancouver and working as a carpenter and furniture maker. The focus of the media's reporting at that time was the massive 7.6 magnitude earthquake in Guatemala. It killed over 20,000 people and left over a million people homeless. One Sunday Pastor Bob said a few words about the earthquake and announced that if anyone wanted to donate money to help the earthquake victims, he would find a place to send their donation. But God wanted more from me, and I heard a voice say, ***Go to Guatemala***.

Looking up and then all around me, I asked myself, where did that voice come from? I asked the people in the row behind me and those on either side if they had said something about Guatemala. They looked at me strangely, shrugged and shook their heads. I must have appeared quite confused because now there were several people looking at me with concern. I thought what had happened was inexplicable, so I settled back down to listen to the pastor. I was feeling quite embarrassed when once again I distinctly heard a voice from directly above me say, ***Go to Guatemala***. As soon as the voice started, I turned around quickly to see who could be standing that close to me. But there was nobody there. Again, I asked the people sitting around me, "Who just said 'Go to Guatemala?' You must have heard it?" One person replied, "Man you must be hearing things because nobody said anything."

This was very strange, and I thought to myself, what could it mean? After the service I asked Pastor Bob if I could speak to him in his office. I explained what had happened during the service and I asked him what it could mean. "I don't know," he replied, "I've never heard of anything like that happening." I said, "It had to be God's voice, because nobody else heard the voice and I heard it as clear as I'm hearing your voice now." "Yes, it had to be God," he replied. I told him, "I just took on a major contract to build furniture and signs for a restaurant. And I just bought a brand-new pickup truck and woodworking machinery so I could fulfill the contract. What am I supposed to do? Am I supposed to just sell everything and go to Guatemala?" "I don't know," said Pastor Bob, "I guess so." Since it was clearly God who had spoken to me, those few words from Pastor Bob were all the confirmation needed. I started making plans to go to Guatemala.

I worked 14 to 16 hours a day to quickly finish the furniture contract. My rented house was my workshop, and my small home was filled with tables, benches, signs, piles of sawdust, and a heavy film of wood dust covering everything. As soon as the contract was completed, I sold my pickup truck and most of my tools. By the time I had paid off my truck loan, paid all my bills, and purchased my round-trip airline ticket to Guatemala City, I had $1000 left to my name. Within a few weeks of hearing the audible voice of God I was on my way to Guatemala.

When You're Clueless, Faith is the Best Arrow in Your Quiver

Pastor Bob's church was not focused on evangelism, so it had no missions department, no missions pastor, no missions program, no missionaries. I was flying blind and out of my depth with no idea what to expect or what to do. My entire knowledge of Christianity and the Scriptures consisted solely of what I picked up from four months of church meetings and Bible studies, along with my daily personal Bible reading. I felt completely unqualified for what Jesus had called me to do. But in March of 1976, a long-haired hippy with a backpack, a sleeping bag, a guitar, a toolbox, $1000 cash in my pocket, and no Spanish language skills, arrived at Guatemala City Airport.

Most of the people on the plane were older women on a tour to see the Mayan ruins in Antigua, an ancient city in Guatemala. The customs officials were opening all their handbags and luggage and rifling through everything as the horrified women looked on. It was quite a scene. My turn came and the customs agent just waved me right through. No checking, no opening anything, just a nod and a wave to go ahead. That was a taste of what were to be many such surprise interventions during this incredible journey. It was a year of divine leading and watching Jesus guide my steps. Jesus obviously knew how unqualified, inexperienced, and clueless I was. And so, He made sure that the Holy Spirit was always near for guidance. I'm sure He also had lots of angels watching over me for protection.

The first thing I had to do was to get situated. All I had was a phone number that Pastor Bob was given for a man thought to be doing earthquake relief work in Guatemala. I went first to the currency exchange and when I found a payphone realized I had no idea what coins to put in. As I stood with the coins in my palm I looked up and said, "Jesus, I need some help here." Immediately a man walked up to me, pointed to a coin in my hand, and pointed to the coin slot on the phone. Then he walked off. "Thanks Jesus!" I exclaimed with relief and joy.

I dialed the number and a lady answered speaking Spanish. I replied to her in English. She said something I couldn't understand then the phone went quiet. I had no idea if she had hung up or was coming back so I hung on and waited. A man came on the phone and in English asked, "Who is this?" I told him my name. There was a long silence before he asked, "How can I help you?" "I don't know," I replied. More silence. Then I blurted out,

"Jesus told me to come to Guatemala, so here I am." "Okay," he said, "Find someone to come to the phone and I will give him directions to write down for you. Show it to a taxi driver outside the terminal and he will bring you here." I looked around and saw a man standing nearby. I shook the phone at him and motioned for him to come over to me. When he did, I handed him the phone and he spoke with the man on the other end and wrote down the directions for me. After thanking him excitedly, I headed outside to find a taxi.

Speaking no Spanish at all I couldn't talk to the taxi driver. I gave him the paper with the directions on it and when he asked me questions all I could do was shrug and smile. "No Spanish," I said repeatedly. He shook his head, probably wondering why I would be traveling alone when I didn't know the language. I wanted to tell him, "I'm not alone. Jesus is right here beside me."

When the taxi arrived at the address, I knocked on the door and was invited in. The man I had spoken to on the phone greeted me and asked me what I was there to do. I said I was a carpenter and I had brought some tools with me, and I could help with the earthquake relief efforts. He told me they were rebuilding a village on the other side of the country and there was a truck leaving the next day at five o'clock in the morning to take building materials to the village. He didn't explain anything about what to expect when I got to the village, and I didn't ask. I knew that Jesus had sent me and that He was watching over me. I assumed that He was preparing the way for me and was opening whatever doors needed to be open, and that I should just go through them. The next morning my adventure entered a whole new level.

Jumping into the Deep End of the Pool

Promptly at 5:00 my ride arrived outside the house where I was staying. It was a dump truck driven by a large rough-looking man from Texas named Bill. Bill had driven the dump truck from Texas and was using it to transport construction materials to various sites where homes were being built for earthquake victims. The village we were heading to was called Pasasaguas, about a ten-hour drive complicated by the earthquake damage to the roads and many of the bridges.

We arrived in Pasasaguas in the late afternoon. I was met by a small group of Americans, all Christians. There were two female missionaries, their pastor, and a young guy from Oregon named Jimbo. They were living in two of the small houses they were building for the villagers. A makeshift kitchen area covered by a large tarp had been set up between some trees with a picnic table in the center. The bathroom facilities consisted of an outhouse and buckets of water for hand and face washing and sponge baths. The water in the village was contaminated and unfit for human consumption so purified drinking water was brought in from Guatemala City by the missionaries in 5-gallon plastic bottles. Unfortunately, the contaminated water was the only drinking water source for the villagers. The locals had a greater resistance than we did, yet poor water quality and malnutrition resulted in an astronomical child mortality rate, and the average life expectancy was only in the forties.

The makeshift kitchen with the picnic table became my bedroom after everyone else went to bed. I slept on the wooden table in my sleeping bag. It was extremely uncomfortable, but I was young and eager to serve Jesus and it was all part of the adventure. I knew Jesus had sent me to Guatemala, and I trusted and believed that He was preparing the way before me. I received whatever was offered and available with thanksgiving and joy.

On one of the trips the missionaries made to Guatemala City a much-welcomed canvas tent arrived for me to sleep in. I was so grateful. The tent became my home and office for the rest of that year. The missionaries also brought me a cot to put my sleeping bag on. I then built a small desk from rough lumber, so now I had a place to sleep, write, and study. I felt very much at home.

Pasasaguas was a terribly poor village. There was no employment in the village at all. Traditionally the homes were all made from handmade adobe brick. The roofs were covered with hand-made clay tiles that were fired in a rough kiln. The tiles were laid across wooden poles used as roof rafters. When the earthquake hit, the handmade bricks simply crumbled and the clay roof tiles fell between the wooden rafter poles, with the adobe walls and roof tiles crushing many of the villagers in their beds. The earthquake was devastating and completely flattened or badly damaged all 120 houses in Pasasaguas. The survivors now resided in makeshift shelters as we worked to build adequate housing. The houses we were building were small and very simple. They consisted of one 10 foot x 12 foot room, with two rough framed windows and a rough framed door. All the lumber was rough cut in a small one-blade sawmill across the highway from the entrance to the village. Each male person in the village receiving a house was required to work with us for one month, so we had a constant flow of new workers coming and other workers going.

Jimbo oversaw the construction, and I worked alongside the Guatemalan workers. After three months, Jimbo returned to his home in Oregon. The two lady missionaries also went back to the USA and their pastor went back to Guatemala City. Because I had elected to stay to finish the reconstruction work, I was the only foreigner left in the village.

Losing my translators left me desperate. I was focused on the construction work and there had been no opportunity for me to study the language. I picked up a few words of Spanish, and a few phrases to use with the workers, but I was far from conversational. One of the missionaries had told me about a three-week intensive Spanish study course in the city of Quetzaltenango, but at $300 the course was expensive and would eat into the limited funds I had. I had no idea how long I would be staying in Guatemala, but I knew that my visa and return trip airline ticket were good for a year. I expected to be there until my year was up or my money ran out. Recognizing language fluency was now required to oversee the construction project, and more importantly, realizing I needed to be able to speak the language to tell the villagers about Jesus, I went to Quetzaltenango.

The language school was designed for total immersion. For three weeks I spent 6 days a week, 8 hours a day, sitting across a desk from a university student. No English was allowed! I had a new teacher each week. Even better, I stayed in the home of a Guatemalan family who spoke no English. I spent every evening after dinner reading the Spanish New Testament. I would look up every word that I didn't know in a Spanish/English dictionary. With a great many words to look up it was slow going.

Amazingly I became quite fluent in those three weeks. Thank you, Jesus! I was fluent in using the vocabulary that I learned, but I did not 100% understand everything that was spoken to me. When I got back to the village the villagers were in awe that someone who didn't speak any Spanish at all could return in only three weeks speaking their language. Admittedly, I was shocked and amazed myself. I recognized that I had been given a special anointing for the language, *especially* when I was speaking to people about Jesus.

Things really changed for me once I became somewhat fluent. Now I could share Jesus with the villagers! Immediately I began to do the work of an evangelist, though I had no prior teaching or training on preaching the gospel. All I knew was that Jesus had saved me from the punishment for my sins and I had to tell everyone I met so that they too could be rescued from their sins and receive eternal life.

I began to preach in the little church that the missionaries and their pastor had built. I also held some evening services and Bible studies at the church, always preaching the gospel of salvation and inviting people to be saved. During those days I lived and breathed Scripture. Though my parents did not believe in Jesus, still I filled my letters to them with Scripture so they would hear the Word of God.

I had never preached in a church before, nor had any training on teaching the Bible, so I just started reading verses from the Bible aloud and then talking about them. I had no commentaries or study guides, something that might be considered a disadvantage. However, I saw that as an advantage, since Jesus through the Holy Spirit was able to speak freely through me without me having any preconceived ideas of what the Scriptures meant.

I am an extreme introvert and was never comfortable speaking to strangers or groups. I did love telling people about Jesus though, so there was no stopping me from doing just that. Something was compelling me to speak about Jesus and His salvation, and my introversion was irrelevant, so awkwardness and discomfort soon became my new normal. It was just part of the package, and the Holy Spirit was able to move freely through me to open Scripture as I preached.

When Jimbo and the other missionaries returned to the USA, they left me with a bit of canned food and drinking water. I had no vehicle and there were no grocery stores in the village, so I knew food and water were soon going to be a problem. I was befriended by Leon, who was considered the richest man in the village because he owned an old flatbed truck. The group that was supplying the materials for the reconstruction project hired Leon and his truck to bring the wood from the sawmill, and to transport the prefabricated walls we built and other materials to each house site. Aware of my predicament, Leon invited me to eat with his family. Our meals consisted of locally grown black beans and corn tortillas, nothing else. Having a wife and six kids already, one more mouth to feed was not a big problem. I paid him $10 a week and my food problems were solved. But the drinking water problem was going to need another solution.

Experiencing a New Level of Faith

Not long after returning from the Quetzaltenango language school I was close to running out of water. The village water was not an option without risking my life. I had been warned upon my arrival to NEVER drink the water from the village water system. It came from a shallow open cistern with no filtering or chemical treatment and was infested with amoebas and other parasites. I was informed that this strain of amoebas causes amoebic dysentery which is very difficult to treat and is sometimes fatal when your heart and lungs become infiltrated.

One day while working on the roof of one of the houses, I saw an old woman approaching; she was carrying a glass of lemonade. We had recently built her a house. She waved and smiled at me, and I knew that she was bringing the lemonade as a thank you for building her a new home.

I found myself in a real dilemma. The town was dirt poor. I knew that it was a huge sacrifice for this woman to obtain a lemon and a little sugar to make the lemonade. She was obviously very grateful, and I knew refusing the gift would break her heart and I didn't want to do that. Looking to heaven I said, "Lord Jesus, I know this glass of lemonade could kill me, but how can I refuse this woman? I am going to drink it and trust You. It's Your problem now."

I came down off the roof as the woman arrived. She handed me the glass of lemonade with a gracious smile. I drank it down heartily and thanked her for her kindness and generosity. By that evening I had fallen ill and spent the entire night and into the early hours of the morning in my little outhouse throwing up, followed by endless dry heaving. I had never been that sick to my stomach in my life. Eventually I fell asleep for a couple of hours and awoke feeling great!

I quickly realized that what had happened that night was more than just me being sick from the water. Jesus had done something to my system! I had asked Jesus to deal with the contaminated water problem and He had handled the problem miraculously. I was filled with faith. Within a few days the last of the filtered water ran out. I knew what to do and began to drink the village water, trusting that Jesus would protect me. The water was truly disgusting. It was a yellowish color full of floating particles, and the odor was foul, but I drank that water every day for the next eight months and I never got sick from it again.

Being Blessed by Being Schooled

In the evenings I would join the village men around the fire. We discussed various topics and I would often speak to them about Jesus, play my guitar, and sing worship songs. Leon approached me one day to discuss "something serious." Apparently by joining in on their political discussions I had gravely upset some of the villagers to the point of threatening violence against me. I was very surprised to hear that there were people in the village who wanted to kill me. I quickly agreed to no longer participate in their political discussions. I added, "Please express my thanks to them for not killing me, but please understand that I will still speak about Jesus. That I cannot stop even if they want to kill me for it." "Oh no," Leon said, "we don't want you to stop talking about Jesus, we enjoy that. Just no more politics."

Chapter 6

Returning to a Divided Home

I had been in Guatemala for almost a year and 120 homes had been built, one for every family in the village. My open-ended ticket was soon to expire and, as I was almost out of money, I left to return home. When I got home I had exactly 11 cents in my pocket.

My first visit was with Pastor Bob and my old church, during which he offered me a job doing maintenance for the church. This gave me some income right away and I rented a room in the house of a family who attended the church.

During my absence a prominent leader in the Shepherding Movement joined the church leadership, pushing himself into a position of authority over Pastor Bob. The church was unsettled and divided over the changes. The basic premise of the movement taught that God worked through a hierarchy structure with a few chosen leaders at the top. Other leaders submitted to them, who in turn had other lesser leaders submitted to them, who had their congregation members submitting to them, and so on. Except for those at the top, everyone was supposed to have someone in authority over them to whom they submitted and took instructions. Instructions that supposedly came directly from God. By the time I returned from Guatemala nearly half the congregation had left the church. Former friends and family were divided, and there were many with wounded hearts.

Being relatively new to Christianity, let alone its myriad of denominations, I naturally had no experience or discernment to effectively assess what had happened to the church. However, I began to better understand the new church dynamics after meeting, dating, and proposing to the church's secretary. Upon learning of this, the new pastor informed me that he and the elders would need to approve all life decisions before I made them. He added that before proposing marriage I should have first consulted with my "shepherd," who he informed me was the man whose house I was staying in. All of this was news to me!

I questioned whether such a teaching was in keeping with what we read in the Bible. He was not interested in discussing my scriptural concerns or point of view and merely explained that I was obligated to obey all instructions from my shepherd since it was his job to hear the will of God *for me*. I explained that although I understood the wisdom of asking for prayer and advice, I saw nothing in the Bible about someone else hearing from God for me and making my important life decisions.

To make sure my thinking was correct I searched through the entire New Testament, not finding anything that supported the doctrines embraced by the Shepherding Movement. To the contrary I found the following scripture: *But Jesus called them (His disciples) to Himself and said, "You know that the rulers of the Gentiles lord it over them, and those who are great exercise authority over them. Yet it shall not be so among you; but whoever desires to become great among you, let him be your servant. And whoever desires to be first among you, let him be your slave—just as the Son of man did not come to be served, but to serve, and to give His life a ransom for many."* [Matthew 20:25-28].

As a maintenance employee I attended all the church's staff meetings. At one of the staff meetings the new pastor announced: "Garry will be the leader of a new house fellowship group." Maybe he thought the way to get me on board with the shepherding doctrine and to assure my compliance was to place me in a position of authority over others. He must have assumed that because he and all the leaders under his control coveted their positions of authority that gave them control over others, I would likewise want to be in the same position. He misjudged me by a country mile! He may have viewed my objections as a power struggle, though I saw it simply as obedience to Jesus and His Word. After the meeting I told him that he was exceeding his authority by announcing me as the leader of a new home fellowship group without first discussing it with me.

The church secretary and I were married during this time, and since we both felt the same about what was happening there, it wasn't long before we also left the church. The experience of seeing the church dividing over the false doctrine of the Shepherding Movement felt like a betrayal. I had come to know a God who was personal and who spoke to me and directed me. But the church leaders wanted me to follow a man who would be my shepherd and would be the voice of God to me. I already had a shepherd, the Great Shepherd Jesus. It was such a disappointment to my heart and soul to learn that the church which had led me closer to Jesus was now straying from His truth.

I was a new believer with only a couple of months' experience as a member of a church congregation. It was very hurtful and disturbing to watch the church and families break apart over the leadership embracing and teaching this false doctrine. This led to a total distrust of churches and leaders who would place human pride and power before Biblical teaching. This distrust led to a welling of righteous anger and indignation in me. Sadly, my righteous anger led to a self-righteous decision, one which I deeply regretted in later years. *I vowed to Jesus that I would never set foot in a church building again except for weddings and funerals.* Unfortunately, I kept this vow for over 20 years.

In retrospect, that promise I made to Jesus was not wise. It was self-righteous indignation that led to possibly one of the worst decisions I ever made in my life. Instead of making such an unreasonable promise, I should have sought out a church that was more Biblically based in its teaching. But I was too young in the Lord to know what was best for me. Feeling such a sense of betrayal, I wanted no further part in organized religion. Many years later, after Jesus called me to serve Him again, I was slightly comforted after reading that most of the leaders of the Shepherding Movement at some point had repented of their involvement in promoting those unbiblical teachings. However, I wish I had heard about that before spending 20 years straying from the path of following Jesus in a setting of Christian fellowship, and instead falling into a life dominated by sin.

Chapter 7

Losing Fellowship: The Backsliding Decades

My misguided self-righteous vow was made in 1977 and I did not set foot in a church again for worship until 1996. For that 20-year period I was clearly enmeshed in a backslidden lifestyle. While I clung to my faith in Jesus like a drowning man clinging to a life preserver, I had no fellowship with other Christians, and by 1996 I had drifted so far away from following Jesus that I did not even own a Bible anymore.

A Miracle to Show He is Still with Me

Though no longer in fellowship with Jesus during this time, He remained faithful and watchful over me. One day my wife and I were blessed to see the protecting hand of Jesus miraculously save us from a potentially deadly car accident while driving down Marine Drive in Vancouver. A car suddenly made a left hand turn right in front of us. The driver never even saw us! I hit my horn and the driver stopped dead in front of us instead of getting out of the way.

Now I should tell you about the van we were driving because it further validates the miracle. It was a 1961 Ford Econoline van. It didn't run well; it didn't always start; it didn't even have seatbelts. The front end was bashed up from an accident and the passenger door had a two-inch gap that was stuffed with old wool socks in the winter to keep us from freezing. The van was in such bad shape that a friend sold it to me for $1! It was in this rickety and undeniably precarious van that we found ourselves about to collide with the car dead stopped in our path only several feet away.

I slammed on the brakes, yelling loudly, "Jesus, Help!" In an instant, without any screeching of tires, without any slipping or sliding or skidding, the van immediately came to a stop. It seemed to even pull backwards a bit when it stopped. My wife was amazed and said, "What just happened?" "Jesus," was my reply.

After the close call we talked about how impossible it was for the van to stop like that. I joked that there must have been quite a few angels hanging onto the back bumper, dragging their feet and pulling with all their might to stop us. More likely, Jesus just spoke the word "stop" to the van since you can't go from 45 mph to dead stopped in a mere moment. Without a doubt we had experienced His miracle and desire to watch over and protect us.

Becoming the King of Pain

In late 1978 I decided that I wanted to become a professional classical guitarist. I had been playing the guitar since I was 12 years old and really loved it. I found a local guy to teach me who was a very good classical guitarist who performed concerts. I took lessons from him once a week and practiced about six hours a day. I got up early every day and practiced for about two hours before work. I practiced for another four hours after work and into the evening. But I ended up with intense pain in my left hip from sitting in the same position for so long. It got so bad that I could no longer play for extended periods. I literally limped away from any potential for a classical guitar career.

Since leaving the church I had eleven different jobs, mostly in construction, furniture making, and carpentry. I began experiencing extreme pain in my chest and spine, compounding the hip pain from the brief stint as a classical guitarist. I was eventually forced to also end my carpentry career and look for work that didn't require heavy labor.

I spent one day working at a used car dealership, but they were so dishonest that I quit after the first day. Soon after, I worked for Sears as a salesperson in their home improvement department where I was involved in designing kitchens and selling kitchen cabinets. Before long I was hired by Sear's installation contractor, who also owned a kitchen cabinet showroom. Then I was hired by a cabinet manufacturer in their factory showroom. The kitchen cabinet market in Vancouver was extremely competitive but I focused on the very high end of the market and did quite well.

By early 1979 the initial hip pain had turned into almost constant extreme pain in both hips, my back, chest, and neck. I went to many doctors to try to get a proper diagnosis for the pain I was experiencing, yet test after test came back negative. They could not find a cause for my pain, and since the medical doctors failed to find the source of the pain it was assumed to be psychological. The pain, however, was very real, so I sought alternative approaches from chiropractors, acupuncturists, holistic doctors, etc. All of them promised me relief, yet none could deliver. It was extremely frustrating to be in such extreme pain while no one believed it was real or could not help alleviate my misery.

It was not until more than ten years later when I was in my late thirties that my pain was finally diagnosed. A condition in my eyes led a doctor to diagnose me with Reiter's Syndrome. A blood test showed that I have a very distinctive genetic marker called the HLAB27 antigen. The test results indicated ankylosing spondylitis (AS), a condition closely associated with that genetic marker. Finally, the reason for my pain had been identified. AS is an extremely rare condition that causes inflammation of the soft tissue in the body which results in extreme pain. Worse news followed; there was no cure. In fact, the doctor noted there was no effective treatment for the pain. Since it was a degenerative disease, the expectation was that it would get progressively worse. I was told to expect further complications including a related condition, Crohn's disease. The doctor's prognosis proved 100% accurate a few years later when I contracted Crohn's. And while I was relieved to discover the cause and source of this daily misery, it did not help me manage the pain which continued to lead my life like a steer with a ring in its nose.

Not Just Any Old Car Crash

In 1981 I was hired by my dad to help complete the construction of a golf course in Whistler by the contractual deadline, and then to work in his land development company on an ongoing basis. I left my highly lucrative job selling kitchens in Vancouver and my wife and I moved to Squamish, the town where I was born. I was commuting forty miles to Whistler for work. It was during one of my daily commutes that I had a profound near-death experience—and quite possibly a momentary actual death.

One day I was driving home from Whistler after work, and it was raining hard. I was driving my mom's car doing about 50 mph around a curve in the road when my left rear tire blew. The car immediately hydroplaned on the wet road, swerving violently, and spinning completely around. The car was now careening backwards and completely out of control. Hitting a large boulder on the side of the road, it flipped end-over-end down the highway. It then rolled onto its side repeatedly until going off the edge of the road, rolling down a 30-foot rock embankment and finally landing in a river.

During those brief moments (which did not feel brief at the time) I was being violently bashed about inside the car. Since I was not wearing a seatbelt, it was purely God's protection that kept me inside the car. When the post between the front and back seats collapsed into the car and violently hit the side of my head, I realized I was severely hurt. After more severe blows to my head, I thought, "My head is being bashed in and I am dying."

The pain stopped suddenly even though I was still being violently thrown about. Then I experienced the sensation of being thrust out of my body and I cried out, "Jesus, here I come." In the next moment I had the feeling of being pulled back into my body. Then I had the distinct sensation that you would feel if someone took a large barrel of warm oil and poured it over your head. I could feel the warm liquid running down my head, then down my body all the way down to my feet. I assumed it was blood pouring from my head and that my head had been split open from the violent impacts. The strange sensation made me feel warm and safe, satisfied and content, and, curiously, loved. I was overcome with complete peace, which was clearly out of place considering my situation, but it permeated my entire being. I assumed I was dead, and I was so looking forward to seeing Jesus face to face.

The car was now violently rolling downwards, causing more blows to my head. Finally, there was a loud metallic crunching sound, and the car came to rest in the river. All was quiet and I felt no pain for the first time in many years. As I looked up at the sky with the car roof pushed over to the right, I wondered: "Why am I sitting still here in the car if I am dead?" Standing up on the car seat and then on the driver's door I jumped onto the large rocks on the side of the river. Bounding up the rock embankment I stood at the top looking down in wonder at the car.

I was very confused. I looked for blood and felt my head for the wounds I knew must be there, but there were none. There was only a small cut on my finger where my wedding ring had been caught when the driver's door caved in against the steering wheel. The surprising possibility that I could still be alive suddenly hit me. I reflected on the sensation I had of warm blood running down my body and now thought it must have been Jesus healing my head wounds and anointing me back to life. I was genuinely disappointed when I realized I was still alive. I looked up and said, "Jesus, why in the world would You save my life? I'm no use to You here. I'm the guy who has lived in constant pain and wants to die, so why would You go to all that effort to save me like this?" Little did I know how prophetic it was when I said, "Jesus You must have some future plans for my life that I know nothing about."

Minutes later a logging truck stopped when the driver saw me standing on the side of the road soaking wet. I told him I had a car accident. When he asked, "Where is your car?" I pointed down the bank. He walked over to the side of the road and looked down at the river. He let out a gasp and stood there in shock with his mouth hanging open in amazement as he asked, "How in the world did you survive that crash? The car is destroyed!" I replied, "It was Jesus." The logging truck driver went to his truck to get a camera and he took the picture below.

The next day I went to visit my mom and report the destruction of her vehicle. Since I was physically intact, she could not believe it when I told her the car was totaled. We drove to the junk yard in Squamish, and I asked to see the car that was towed out of the river the previous day. The guy replied in a somber voice, "I'm very sorry for your loss." "What loss?" I asked." He answered, "Well, the driver was killed in the crash." "No way! I was the driver," I said, "and as you can see, I'm still alive."

The poor guy looked at me like he was seeing a ghost. "There is no way you were driving that car," he said. "That driver is dead for sure. The car is destroyed, and the post between the front and back windows collapsed into the car right where his head would be." "Nope, still not dead," I replied. My mom was in shock and confused by our conversation. "Let me take you to the car," the guy said. When we rounded a corner and my mom saw her car, she burst into tears and grabbed onto me. She realized that there was no way I could have walked out of that car without being seriously injured or killed. Surely, my life had been spared supernaturally by Jesus. But I was going to wait another 16 years before finding out why He had rescued me.

Chapter 8

Jesus Was Working Hard to Get My Attention

One would think that right about now I'd be looking back over the past 4 years and see a pattern. But I did not. Whether it was stubbornness borne from my self-righteous anger toward the church, or maybe just too fearful to recognize that Jesus had clearly been shutting doors right and left, it simply did not occur to me to seek out another Pastor Bob and church. I have been asked this question many times, but simply can't understand why I chose to just remain on the path I was on and not look for an alternative. No doubt it would have helped me to understand what was happening in my life at that time if I had a church for fellowship. The only thing I can surmise in hindsight is that He must have known that I was not "refined and sharpened" sufficiently enough for His future purposes, and so He did not reveal His plans for me.

Moving to the USA

A recession that year put my dad's land development project on hold, and I no longer had work. There were no other jobs for me in Whistler or Squamish, so we were forced to sell our house. We took a huge loss on the house, losing all our savings, and ending up in debt to the Canadian Income Tax Department.

My wife and I returned to Vancouver in 1982 where I went back to work designing and selling kitchen cabinets. I was immediately successful selling kitchens again. I worked 12 to 14 hours a day to put us back on our feet. However, the recession lingered, and a lot of competition in the kitchen design field induced me to consider a move to the USA. With dreams of better economic opportunities and the hope that a warmer climate would ease the extreme pain in my body, I flew to Southern California to check things out. I interviewed with multiple companies, all of whom offered me a job on the spot. My wife and I reduced our possessions to ten small packing boxes of clothing and personal items, which we shipped ahead, and in 1986 we flew to California where I re-started my kitchen design career in America.

Los Angeles had a strong demand for high-end kitchens and within a year I was able to open my own kitchen showroom, Showcase Kitchens. The kitchen business was booming. Typically, I would have between 10 and 20 kitchen remodel projects in production at the same time, requiring me to work very long hours 7 days a week. Success proved costly—in several ways.

Addiction Was Not the Answer

By the late 1980's I was in so much pain from the ankylosing spondylitis that it was all I could do to get up in the morning and go to work. Then a poor decision compounded my problems immensely. Though I had used mind altering drugs in my youth, I had stayed away from hard drugs. In Los Angeles I discovered that almost everyone I knew in the kitchen business was using cocaine. I managed to avoid cocaine for a couple of years, but one evening I was visiting a fellow kitchen designer when he pulled out some cocaine and offered me some. I declined but he challenged me to at least try it once. I was admittedly curious, and since it seemed that everyone I met was doing it, I agreed to give it a try. Big foolhardy mistake!

I have since learned that I have an addictive personality and so "just once" was the beginning of my cocaine addiction. I became utterly addicted to cocaine even as it slowly destroyed the little remaining health of my body, my mind, my business, and my marriage. My wife divorced me and moved back to Canada, but still my cocaine use increased. After about six months I came to the realization that I had to stop using cocaine immediately and forever or else lose my business and end up bankrupt or dead.

Quitting cocaine was the hardest thing I have ever done. I went cold turkey. I had to get rid of the phone numbers of everyone I knew who sold cocaine. And I had to tell all my friends to never offer it to me again. I stopped going to places where people sold cocaine, and I stopped hanging out with friends who I knew were using it. Still, every single day for over two years, I yearned for the drug. I really have no idea how I survived my cocaine addiction or where the strength came from to kick it. Not from me, I was a mess. Jesus and His angels must have been working hard to keep me alive as it was truly miraculous that I did not overdose and die. But despite my backslidden state, Jesus clearly had a plan for my life and dying of a cocaine overdose was not in that plan.

The Final Solution

By 1993 the pain was so extreme I knew I could not continue living with it much longer. I was walking with a permanent limp because of the crippling pain in my hips, and I had so much pain in my spine, hips and neck that I simply could not tolerate it anymore. I often thought of killing myself to stop the pain. Over the years I had seen well over a hundred medical professionals: doctors, specialists, chiropractors, acupuncturists, wholistic practitioners, nutritionists, and therapists, both in Canada and the USA. Nothing they suggested or tried had helped.

For the next few years I continued to struggle, trying to manage life with the pain, but becoming increasingly crippled with time.

The pain had gone far beyond intolerable. At times I was fully in awe of how much pain I was going through, and I was truly shocked that my body was still functioning. Apparently, no level of pain will just outright kill you. Instead, it slowly breaks the person, physically, mentally, and emotionally.

It was now 1996 and it had become increasingly difficult to deal with employees or to be in a relationship. I was constantly on the edge of losing it emotionally. The ordeal of trying to deal with extreme pain caused me to push people away from me. Eventually it became impossible to maintain any emotional balance at work and it became increasingly difficult to run my business. The only solution I could see to stop the unbearable physical and emotional pain was to end my life, so I decided to commit suicide. I closed my business and moved to a small town called Julian. I intended to spend a couple of months resting and making peace with God before I ended my life.

I spent the time at Julian relaxing, thinking, and reading. Spiritually I was clinging to my faith in Jesus. Though I trusted Jesus for my salvation, I worried whether my ongoing sin might disqualify me from heaven. I understood salvation well. Back in 1977 I was preaching salvation to others in Canada and Guatemala. But over the years since then I had fallen far away from following and obeying Jesus. At times, in despair I would say a quick prayer to Jesus. Those prayers always went something like this, "Jesus You know that I love You, and I do believe that You died for my sins and rose from the dead. But I know what Your Word says, and I have not been following You at all for a very long time. I am so steeped in sin that it is scary. I've tried many times and I can't change, so if You have to send me to hell when I die, I will understand. I will simply worship You forever from hell." I know now that it was an insane prayer, but the constant extreme pain had negatively impacted my thinking. I was so backslidden that those words were all that was left in my heart to pray.

Chapter 9

Jesus Spoke to Me Through a Butterfly

I was in so much constant pain that every evening I would sit in my jetted tub and read for hours. I figured that since I was going to die soon, I would try to make peace with God. I also spent a lot of time outside walking and thinking. The monarch butterflies were migrating to Mexico and a swarm of them stopped in my yard to visit the flowers. While walking through the garden one day, my mind immersed in a myriad of questions, I bent down to study one of the butterflies in detail. In my mind it was as though I could see the butterfly on a molecular level. I could see that this tiny creature was designed and made with amazingly intricate detail, details which only provided elegance and beauty, but not needed for its survival. It was then that I realized how involved God is in creating and giving life in an amazingly beautiful way to something as simple and seemingly insignificant as a butterfly. I was so moved that I cried out loud, "God, You are involved in the minutest details of Your creations! How much are You involved in my own life that I don't understand?" I was overwhelmed with a sense of how great and wonderful God is, and I felt that something was about to change.

Born Again - Again

A few days later while relaxing in the tub, I suddenly heard a voice speak to me. It was a voice that I had not heard for 20 years. It was not an outward audible voice like the voice that had told me to go to Guatemala. Rather I heard a very clear voice internally, an inner knowing. It was the voice of my Jesus that I recognized even after all these years.

Jesus gently asked, "Garry, you are planning to kill yourself, aren't you?" "Yes," I immediately responded. "I have no choice. I am in way too much pain, both physically and mentally. I can't take it anymore." Jesus spoke, "Before you do that, I want to use your life to tell others about My salvation."

"Me?" I questioned in total surprise. "You must be kidding! It's been 20 years since I have heard Your voice, but I recognize Your voice and I still know who You are. And I don't mean to be disrespectful, but You must have me mistaken with someone else, someone who is holy. Jesus, You have seen how I have lived the past 20 years. There is no way that You could think that I am worthy of serving You. I can't possibly be of any use to You." "I know all that," He replied. "But if you are willing, I can change you and I can use your life to tell others about My salvation."

I was in total confusion, and I blurted out, "Ok. If You are serious, I will do it. I will go anywhere You ask me to go, and I will do anything You ask me to do, but on one condition." I could imagine Him laughing for setting a condition, but He responded to me kindly and He asked me, "And what is that one condition?" I replied, "Like I said, I will go anywhere and do anything You ask, but only if You will agree to tell me clearly where You want me to go and what You want me to do. Because if You don't tell me clearly, I will sit here and do nothing. If You agree to that, then I will agree not to kill myself and I will tell others about Your salvation." "Deal," was the one word reply that I heard. Then He added, "By the way, that woman you are with, you marry her." And with that the conversation was over.

I was in shock, but I was energized like never before. I had no idea how I was going to accomplish anything in my condition, but I knew one thing. If Jesus wanted me to serve Him in the physically and emotionally crippled state that I was in, then how I was going to accomplish that was going to be His problem.

I bought a Bible and spent many hours reading through the New Testament. I devoured the Word of God like a starving man sitting down to a delicious meal. I was so convicted of having lived my own sinful ways for 20 long years that I knew I had to start all over again. One night I took myself through the Biblical process of repenting and asking Jesus to forgive all my sins and committing to following and serving Him. I once again declared Jesus as my Savior and Lord and I confessed my belief that God had raised Him from the dead. I was born again, again.

I was elated that Jesus had visited me and spoken to me, and that He wanted to use my life to serve Him. That night I started a journey that continues after 28 years. That journey has been a battle at times, and satan and his demons have made multiple attempts to stop me from sharing the message of salvation with lost sinners. But Jesus has been faithful, often moving miraculously to fulfill His plan for me.

Chapter 10

Walking with Jesus Once Again

While reading the Bible I came to the scripture that said we should not forsake the gathering of the people of God, and I realized I needed to find a church. I had been forsaking the gathering of Christians for 20 years.

The Sunday Turkey Choir

Because of my past relationship with the structured church, I struggled with the thought of returning. So, one Saturday night I prayed for peace of mind: "You know the decision I am struggling with Lord. Church starts tomorrow at 10:00, so if I am to go to church, wake me at 8:30." I sleep poorly because of the pain, with deep sleep typical in the morning and I was in the habit of sleeping quite late. My bedroom was on the top floor of a three-level house and the door to the balcony overlooking the backyard is open at night for the cool fresh air.

In the morning I was suddenly awakened by a loud and strange racket coming from the yard. I looked over at the clock and it was 8:30. Not 8:29 and not 8:31. Exactly 8:30. Walking out onto the balcony to see what the commotion was, I saw a flock of about 20 wild turkeys standing in a semi-circle facing the balcony, all gobbling and cackling in a loud shrill. There were always wild turkeys in the area, and I would see them nearly every day, but I had never witnessed this type of behavior.

I watched the turkeys staring up at me while still creating their noisy cacophony. "You have got to be kidding me?" I said out loud. "You can even do this Lord?" I laughed. I had already felt led to the town's non-denominational church and was readying myself to leave when the doubts started. What if the turkey song was just a coincidence? I worried I hadn't really heard from Him.

I talked myself out of going to church that day. All week there was nothing unusual about the turkeys' behavior. I spent a lot of time that week pondering what had happened on Sunday, and I continued to struggle with the decision of going to church or not. The next Saturday night, as I was going to bed, I challenged Jesus again saying, "If You want me to go to church tomorrow, do it again." The next morning, I was awoken by the same commotion. I bolted up and shouted, "No way!" I looked at the clock and it was exactly 8:30 on the dot. I went to the balcony, looked down, and there they were again, only the flock was much larger today. The turkeys were again standing in a semi-circle facing the balcony and looking straight up at me and cackling at the top of their voices. "Okay, You win, I got the message." I said to Jesus.

The church service was amazing. I had not experienced corporate worship for 20 years. Frankly, I had not done any personal worship during that time either. When worship began, I was emotionally overwhelmed and I wept all through the worship. It was like a dam had broken in me; I felt like every single cell in my body was worshipping Jesus. I was undone. Being extremely introverted, I didn't talk to anyone at first. But after several weeks the pastor and several others from the congregation welcomed me. Before long I was attending a mid-week Bible study and playing guitar on the worship team.

I was so in love with Jesus. I was on fire and wanted to share with others about His love and message of salvation. I quickly became once again familiar with the Bible verses that speak about salvation, and everywhere I went I spoke to everyone I knew about Jesus. He was preparing me for the next assignment.

Getting Married Again

When I moved to Julian I had purposely distanced myself from my girlfriend/fiancé. I did not want her to suffer when I ended my life, as was the initial plan. After my encounter with Jesus and the turkey choir clock, I had to talk to her, so I invited her to Julian for the weekend and told her what had happened. She had never had a born-again experience (she was a lapsed Catholic), so my experience likely seemed incredulous to her.

I explained my promise to completely follow Jesus and that would mean going anywhere He directed and doing whatever He asked me to do. Since He halted my suicide, I knew I was on borrowed time. I suspected He would send me to dangerous places, and I figured I might not survive. I clearly explained I intended to be obedient to His call and wanted her to understand that she could never question where Jesus sends me. Nor could she argue with me about it. I explained that Jesus is first in my life, and I am going to obey whatever He tells me to do. I warned her that at times it would be very difficult for her. Then I said, "If you want to stay with me and get married, you will have to agree with all that. But my advice to you is to run, as far and as fast as you can away from me."

Surprisingly she chose to stay with me and soon after our wedding I explained the gospel to her, and my wife was saved and baptized. I also was baptized again since I had spent 20 years in a backslidden condition. True to her word, my wife has never questioned or argued with me about going anywhere that Jesus has asked me to go. She will sometimes ask me, "Are you sure you have heard from Jesus on this?" But she has always supported me if I have sought direction from Jesus first.

Chapter 11

Obedience Training Trips with Jesus

It was only a few weeks after getting married that I felt the Lord leading me to the mission field. Admittedly I had been eagerly looking forward to hearing from Him and learning where He was sending me and what His plan was to serve Him. The first opportunity came when I was introduced to a Christian Organization that had a medical ministry.

The Dominican Republic

A mission trip was leaving soon to the Dominican Republic and there was room on the team for one more. I asked Jesus, and He confirmed I was to go by opening the door wide for me to go through. Within a couple of weeks, I was on my way to the Dominican Republic to accompany a team of Christian Doctors and their assistants on a medical mission.

The director was a kind elderly man. He was a doctor who really loved Jesus and he loved to serve people with few or no options for good medical treatment. He was also the team leader and served with a wonderful group of people. It was such a joy to travel and serve with them. When they needed a pharmacist for the team, they asked the group if anyone had any experience. I jokingly told them I had a lot of prior experience with drugs, so they put me in charge of the pharmacy!

Unfortunately, I had not spoken Spanish for 20 years and had long forgotten most of it. Although I was able to fill the prescriptions the doctors wrote, my ability to share the gospel was not happening. I passed out Spanish tracts and New Testaments but couldn't explain the gospel message to the patients directly, so one of the medical team was needed to translate. The language difficulty was frustrating, but I was able to interact and serve with some wonderful people.

Hermosillo, Mexico

Almost immediately after returning from the Dominican Republic I heard that Pastor Mike Macintosh, an evangelist who pastored a Calvary Chapel Church in San Diego, was organizing a two-day mission trip to Hermosillo, Mexico. Teams would be working in various parts of the city during the days. Pastor Mike would preach and share the gospel at night at a big event in the main stadium where all the locals would be invited.

The first day was very active. We went to a small community quite a distance from Hermosillo city center. My group performed a puppet show, another group did face painting, crafts, and other activities for the younger kids. Still others did sports such as soccer and volleyball for the older kids. It was incredible and beautiful to watch all the people who had come to serve interacting with the villagers. After our puppet show I questioned the team leader, "When do we share the gospel with the people here?" "We don't," he replied. "Pastor Mike will do that at the event this evening." I responded, "But, these people are many miles from where they will hold the event. They don't have cars and they don't have money. How will they get to the event?" He merely shrugged in reply.

I was distraught and couldn't believe we weren't going to share the gospel after spending so much time, money, and effort to get there. Was this to be just an exercise in entertaining the lost? Between puppet shows I thoughtfully watched the crowd and noticed a young lady from our large group walking through the crowd with a Spanish Bible and talking to different people. I knew what she was doing wasn't part of the planned program. This woman had taken the initiative to evangelize! She obviously spoke Spanish fluently and I watched her conversing with different people. She would read to them from her Bible and at some point they would bow their heads as she prayed with them before moving on to speak with someone else.

She was sharing the gospel with many and I was very moved by what I saw. I wanted to share Jesus also, since there were far too many people for her to reach alone. In prayer I cried out to Jesus to help me share the gospel with these people. That evening my prayer was answered by the inspiration to prepare a plan for witnessing.

Unfortunately, though I learned Spanish while in Guatemala, I had not spoken the language since then and I could only remember a few greeting words. A small pocket English/Spanish dictionary and some Spanish New Testaments were all I had to assist me. I had marked the verses in my Bible that I always used when sharing the gospel, and I marked those same verses in the Spanish New Testament. 14 verses were marked, also a salvation prayer and several questions and responses were translated into Spanish.

The questions and responses I translated went like this: "Do you know what the Bible says about Jesus and salvation?" "Can I tell you what the Bible says about Jesus and salvation?" "Would you like to repent of your sins and ask Jesus to forgive your sins and save you from the punishment of hell and fill you with the Holy Spirit?" Then I also translated the answer that I would have to give whenever anyone asked me a question: "I'm sorry but I don't understand Spanish, so I don't know what you are saying. Would you like me to continue?" It took me several hours to write it all down and then practice speaking the verses, the questions and responses, and the salvation prayer. Finally, I was ready and went to bed.

The next day after our group performed their first puppet show, I asked Steve, one of the brothers in the puppet group, to please pray for me. Steve is a man filled with faith and joy and the Holy Spirit. "I need prayer badly," I said. "I'm going to go and share the gospel with some of these people." Steve looked at me curiously and said, "But I thought you don't speak Spanish?" "I don't, that's why I need your prayers." Steve shook his head with a big smile on his face like he thought I was crazy. Then he prayed for me.

I stood up and looked out at the people with whom I was going to share the gospel with. For a moment Jesus let me see His heart for those people and I was consumed with the love that Jesus had for them. I say consumed because I was so emotionally overwhelmed that I started to weep. I thought my heart would break from the depth of emotion stirred up by that kind of love. It only lasted a few seconds. Then I heard Jesus say, "That is how much I love these people." I had never, or since, felt that much compassion and love. I knew it was a very special moment that Jesus was allowing me to experience. A moment that I will never forget for as long as I live. It took me a few minutes to get my emotions back in check. Then I went down the trailer stairs under the influence of the Holy Spirit to preach the gospel in a language that I did not speak anymore.

I started with the first person standing in front of me, a middle-aged man. From the notes I had prepared the night before, I questioned him if he knew what the Bible said about Jesus and salvation. He shook his head and said "no." I then asked if he wanted me to share with him what the Bible said about Jesus and salvation. Fortunately, he responded in the affirmative. I began to read aloud the Spanish verses in the order I had them marked. After each verse I would pause a bit and say a silent prayer asking Jesus for help. I continued reading the 14 verses, and when finished I asked him if he wanted to repent of his sins and trust Jesus for his salvation. He nodded an enthusiastic *"Yes"*, so I led him in a prayer for salvation. I noticed there were tears in his eyes when he had finished praying.

It went so smoothly that I knew Jesus had sent the Holy Spirit to help me. I was ecstatic and in awe that Jesus could use me even when I didn't speak the language. I was praising Him all that day as I saw many people repent and ask Jesus to save them. Steve and I were rejoicing together at the end of the day over the amazing thing that Jesus had done that day. This fruitful trip bolstered my faith that with Jesus all things will be possible to accomplish. Whatever is needed on the mission field, it will be provided. It is the reward for obedience. I was going to need a great deal more faith for the trips that were ahead.

Chapter 12

An Extreme Testing in the Jungle

My next trip was with the same medical ministry that I had accompanied to the Dominican Republic. This trip was to the jungle in Peru to witness to the Machiguenga tribe in a remote village deep in the Amazon. The trip required four different plane rides—two flights to get from San Diego to Lima, then two more to get over the Andes mountains to a small village on the side of the Urubamba River. The remainder of the journey would be a two-day boat trip upriver.

As soon as I heard about this trip, I asked Jesus to confirm that He wanted me to go and I received immediate confirmation for this mission. There would be four other people in the group, a doctor, a nurse, Ken (the ministry leader), and a man from the oil company that had invited us to come. The other four people would be staying in the jungle for about a week. Ken had asked me before our departure if I would be willing to stay in the jungle for an extended trip of up to 30 days to build a school in the remote village, and I agreed. I was told that the oil company would provide a portable sawmill for me to cut lumber from the local trees.

The trip into the jungle was amazing. After we all arrived in Lima, we transferred to a smaller plane which landed in a small airport before climbing aboard an even smaller plane, which seated about 8 people and landed on a dirt landing strip in a very tiny remote village. By afternoon we got into two boats and headed up the Urubamba River in pouring rain. We traveled several hours before stopping at an unoccupied oil workers camp alongside the river to spend the night.

The next morning our journey continued upriver. We had two Peruvian guides, one piloting each boat. They spoke both Machiguenga and Spanish. The river was quite low with rocks and logs jutting up in various places. Sandbars in the middle of the river hindered our progress at times. The guides spent the entire trip with their eyes glued to the river to avoid the rocks, logs, and sandbars. The motor in our boat quit at one point along the way so the driver had to stop and work on it. At another point we hit a rock with the propeller and had to stop again so the driver could remove the propeller and straighten it out. After seven arduous hours we arrived at a small sandbar on the river bank. There was a group of smiling villagers greeting us as we landed.

We walked a short distance from the river and were shown a place in the jungle to set up camp. Of course, there were no hotels, no guest houses, no spare bedrooms, no bathrooms, nor any running water or electricity. For shelter there was an old bamboo platform with a leaky thatched roof where we quickly set up our small one-man tents as darkness was descending rapidly. In the jungle it was hot and extremely humid. I was sweating out all the water I could take in.

The plan was for Ken and the doctor and nurse to hold medical clinics in the village for a couple of days. Then an oil company pilot would helicopter them to a couple of other villages to hold medical clinics. When the other four people left by helicopter to visit the other villages, I asked to see the portable sawmill.

The villagers spoke the Machiguenga language, but a few also spoke some Spanish. I had been studying Spanish every day since the trip to Hermosillo so I could now engage in basic conversations. A man who spoke Spanish took me to see the sawmill. He showed me the site where the school was to be built. There was a tiny shack made from bamboo poles and he pointed to some parts lying against a wall of the shack, stating, "There's the sawmill." I stared in shock at the small pile of stuff lying there. It consisted of an approximately 24″ diameter saw blade, a rolled-up cloth belt, a 12″ piece of round metal with a bolt on one end, and two round plastic bearings. "Where is the rest of it?" I asked. "That's it," he said. "But there is no motor and no support stand!" I responded. "We will use the motor from the boat," he replied. "But what am I supposed to attach the motor and the blade to?" I asked. "I don't know," he replied. "This is all they sent us."

I considered my predicament. I had a blade, a belt, a piece of round steel, and two bearings. I saw no way to use those parts to build a sawmill. There was no stand or base, no lumber to build a stand or base, no screws or nuts and bolts, no guard for the blade, no switch or wiring. How could I possibly build a sawmill with what was there? It was ludicrous! I had expected a fully assembled portable sawmill. But they were expecting me to cut enough lumber to build a school with this. It was simply not possible.

I also had another problem. The humidity level in the jungle was over 100%, a condition called supersaturation. I was sweating so much that within just a couple days I had consumed all the water I had brought, which was two 5-gallon jugs. I thought the ten gallons would last me until I could set up a basic solar water purification system I planned to build. Once the two jugs of water ran out, there was only river water to drink, which was not safe and had to be treated with iodine before drinking.

When Ken and the oil company representative came back with the doctor and nurse, I told Ken there was no sawmill, only a few parts that could not be transformed into a working sawmill. "That's all we have, so you'll have to make it work," Ken said. I objected, explaining there was no conceivable way to make a working sawmill from the parts available. "You need to make the sawmill work, build the school, and leave them a sawmill that they can use after you leave, so they can cut lumber for the village. That is what we promised them," was Ken's response.

"But there is nothing to build a sawmill with!" I said, "Only a couple of pieces that cannot possibly be turned into a useable sawmill." I explained that as a very resourceful person, given enough time, I could probably use bamboo and rope and the boat motor to assemble something that might work to cut up a few boards. But there is no guard for the saw, and there are no bolts or fasteners to secure it. Whatever I build will just come apart, and it will almost certainly happen when the 24″ saw blade is spinning fast. When that happens, someone is going to get badly hurt or killed. Also, if I was to leave such a saw for the villagers to use, someone would cut off their arm for sure. Or the blade will spin loose, mangling anyone in its way. I couldn't in good conscience build something so predictably dangerous.

Ken and the oil company rep had not made the proper preparations for this job. My back was against a wall, and I was being pressured to do what I knew was unconscionably dangerous. I had not come to the jungle to do harm.

I needed to clear my head from the nonsensical demands. As I walked along the jungle trail, I asked Jesus to please help me out of this mess. Almost immediately I saw a large stack of wood in the bush beside the trail. I investigated further and I found that there were multiple piles of prefabricated walls. They were in square sections eight feet high and eight feet wide. Counting the number of walls in the piles, I calculated there was enough there to build the school. I walked back and found the oil company rep, asking him to follow me to the piles of prefabricated walls. He told me the materials belonged to the oil company and were used to build housing for oil workers in the jungle, but he agreed to let me use the walls to build the school.

That same evening something very strange happened. I heard Jesus say to me, "You have to leave here as quickly as possible and get home." Questioning why I had to leave, He didn't reply verbally, but He replied with power. Immediately I lost the sense of His peace about where I was. I had never experienced such a feeling before. It was almost like Jesus removed His presence from me, and I felt like running. I understood that He was making it very clear for me so that I would follow His instructions.

I went to Ken and told him what had happened. "I have no idea why," I said, "but Jesus told me to get home as soon as possible."

"It's just jungle fever," he said, "you'll get over it in a few days."

"No," I said. "You don't understand. I know the voice of Jesus and I know what He said. I need to leave here as soon as possible."

I told him about the prefabricated walls with which I could accomplish the task I came to the jungle to do, then requested his permission to rent one of the boats and the boat drivers to take me down river if I could get the school built within the next two days. He was reluctant, insisting it was just jungle fever, and I was equally as emphatic that it was not and that I had heard from Jesus. Ken finally agreed to let me take the boat and drivers once the school was completed.

A Christ-Guided Amazon Cruise

With the help of the entire village armed with machetes, and within just a couple of hours, what was previously lush thick jungle was neatly cleared to the ground. The people then helped carry the prefab walls to the site and a bunch of the men stayed to help me build the school. By the end of the second day, the school building was finished. The following day I was on my way out of the jungle. I got up early and packed my tent and belongings. I took off in the boat with the two drivers, expecting to arrive at the destination well before dark. The river was dangerous even during the day and most certainly not safe to be on at night. In addition to the rocks and logs sticking up due to the low water level, there were a lot of alligators in the river and on the banks ready to eat us if the boat capsized.

We got about an hour down-river when the motor suddenly started to sputter and then it died. One of the drivers worked on it and got it running again. About 20 minutes later it did the same thing. Once again, he fiddled with it and got it running, but that only lasted for a few minutes before it died yet again. This continued multiple times over several hours until the motor refused to start at all. The boat driver threw up his hands in resignation. We drifted onto a gravelly spot on the riverbank and got out of the boat. I asked what we could do. The drivers just shrugged and one of them said, "We are stuck here until someone comes along. It could be days before anyone comes with a boat large enough to pick us up."

We expected to be in the village before dark, and the day had started out sunny and warm. The boat drivers did not have any gear to spend the night on the riverbank. I had my pack with my tent, but it was a tiny one-man tent and I only had one sleeping bag. We had no food and only a little drinking water, so if we were stuck there for several days we were in big trouble. Also, I needed to make it to the village that night. The only flight for five days was leaving early the next morning. If I missed it, I would have to wait for five days in the village for the next flight out. Jesus had told me to get home quickly so I had to make it!

The drivers sat down on the riverbank looking dejected and worried. I started to pray, telling Jesus that I knew it was His will for me to get home as soon as possible, but we were completely out of options. I told Jesus that since there was nothing I could do, except pray and ask for His help, I considered it to be His problem and not mine and I needed a miracle on His part to get out of the situation. When I had finished praying, I sat down on the riverbank with no idea what was next.

Not even two minutes had passed before we heard the faint sound of a motor coming from upriver. It got louder and louder until suddenly a boat appeared around the bend in the river. Without hesitation an old man steered his boat right over to us. He had a very brief conversation with the drivers that I could not understand since they were speaking in Machiguenga. Then one of the drivers told me to get my stuff out of our boat and put it in the old man's boat. I was told the old man had offered to lend us his boat. Shocked, I asked, "What is he going to do? How will he get home?" The driver replied, "I don't know, but he is letting us take his boat and we will bring it back to him tomorrow. Let's go quickly before he changes his mind."

I was not about to argue since this offer was so divinely inexplicable. What were the chances of an old man showing up just a few minutes after we got stranded? Offering to lend us his boat while he waited on the river bank all night and the better part of the next day with no gear or supplies was hard to fathom. And where did he come from? His boat was slower than ours so if he had been traveling on the river, we should have passed him. It was clear that only Jesus could make such a thing happen. I began to wonder if the man was human and suspected that he must be an angel. How else could he have appeared within minutes of my praying for a miracle from Jesus? And why else would he stop and offer us his boat, leaving himself completely stranded on the bank of the river in the late afternoon. Why didn't he just come with us? He had no provisions, no tent, no bedding, no food or water, no cell phone. And he never asked for money for allowing us to take his boat.

I was praising Jesus for allowing me to experience such a supernatural miracle as I loaded my stuff into the old man's boat. As we set out the old man was standing on the riverbank waving to us with a big smile on his face. By this time, it was late in the afternoon and we still had hours of river travel ahead of us. We didn't get very far before it started to rain. It was not just a little rain, it was torrential. Then it got pitch dark. We were in big trouble. Although it was extremely unsafe for us to continue traveling on the river at night, there was no other choice. We just kept going.

One of the drivers went to the very front of the boat with a flashlight. He was yelling instructions to the other driver on how to maneuver to avoid hitting rocks and logs sticking up out of the river. It was a crazy trip. With pitch darkness and rain falling in torrents, visibility with the flashlight was only a couple of feet in front of the boat. I could see that it was all incredibly stressful for the drivers. However, I was loving every minute of it. I had already seen Jesus do a miracle with bringing the old man and his boat and I was filled to overflowing with faith. I knew beyond any doubt that Jesus was closely watching over my journey, and I felt safe and content. I also knew that if it was His will for me to come home to heaven, then I could drown or be eaten by an alligator that night, but if it was His will for me to make it to the village, there was nothing that could stop us. The drivers must have thought I was out of my mind. They were frantic with worry and concern, and I was sitting there in the boat contentedly smiling and singing praises to Jesus. It was the most awesome feeling. Despite being in such great danger I had complete peace in my heart and mind. I couldn't thank and praise Jesus enough for the peace and joy that was filling me.

It was a harrowing time for the drivers as they shouted panicked instructions to each other over the sound of the motor and the driving rain. Then they told me their newest fear. With the darkness and the torrential rain there was a strong possibility that we would not see the village. We could go right past it in the dark. I prayed while watching the shore for any signs of the village. The drivers continued with their panicked shouting back and forth as we careened down the river. Occasionally we would bounce off submerged trees and scrape the bottom on rocks and sandbars. Finally, one of the drivers shouted in relief as he spotted the village. It was about 1:00 A.M. when we arrived. We made our way to the oil company bunk house and slept the sleep of the exhausted.

Flying Out of the Jungle - A Testimony About Open Doors

In the morning the rain continued, and the valley was completely socked in with thick low clouds. Such low hanging clouds would make it impossible for a plane to land on the tiny airstrip. I was praying continuously that Jesus would open the clouds so the plane could land. I knew that if the plane could not land today the flight would bypass the village, and I could not wait 5 days before the next one. Jesus told me to return home quickly and had provided miraculous provisions thus far and that filled me with faith that the clouds would clear and the plane would land. The weather was clearly not in my favor that day, but by the Spirit I had complete faith that Jesus would provide a path forward.

While waiting at the tiny airstrip, news came from the village that the plane was delayed because the clouds were too thick to land. It started to clear up a bit and we got news that the plane would be on its way soon, but then the clouds again thickened, and another delay was reported. This went on all morning into early afternoon. I was filled with faith and just kept praying for the clouds to open. Later that afternoon news came from the village that the plane had passed us by due to the thick cloud cover; there would be no plane for us today.

I couldn't believe it. I mean I *really* couldn't believe it. There was no way Jesus would tell me to get home quickly, provide those miracles to get me down the river, and then leave me stranded in this village for five days. I stood there for a long time after everyone else left and went to their homes. I simply refused to believe it. I expected the plane to miraculously appear any second out of nowhere, but that didn't happen. Eventually I resigned myself to the fact that there would not be a plane flying out today.

I went to the little restaurant in the village to have a late lunch. They had a big fish hanging from a beam that was caught that morning in the river and they were cutting off filets. I ordered the fish and rice and was enjoying my lunch when some kids came running up to me. "There's a plane coming!" I hurried after the kids back to the airstrip.

At the airstrip we could hear the drone of a plane approaching from the valley. When it emerged from the clouds, we saw that it wasn't the plane expected; it was a Peruvian Airforce plane. As it was landing, I heard someone say that the plane had come to pick up a sick woman who needed to get to a hospital urgently. Then a woman came down the trail being carried on a homemade stretcher. I could tell the plane was large enough to hold about six people, so I walked up to one of the Airforce crew and asked if I could get on the plane. After looking me up and down he agreed to my request.

It was getting dark when we landed at the next airport. I saw a plane on the tarmac starting to taxi down the runway. I knew it had to be going to Lima since it was a large plane. I hurried into the arrival building, praying as I went. As I gave my ID to the guy behind the counter, I asked if he could get me on the plane now at the end of the runway preparing for takeoff. He told me that was not possible. I kept praying, and looking him straight in the eyes I asked again, "Are you sure I can't get on that plane?" It was like a light went off in his head and he perked up excitedly and said, "Let me try." He ran and grabbed a radio and very enthusiastically talked the pilot into turning the plane around to return for me. He appeared very surprised the pilot had agreed to return and he told me to hurry outside. A few minutes later the plane was taxiing down the runway again, only this time with me on board.

The Heart Wrenching Arrival Home

My wife and I had a cat named Jen-a-fur who I loved very much, and she was quite attached to me as well. Jen-a-fur was quite old and in poor health and it was obvious that she might soon pass on to heaven. While preparing for the trip I had asked Jesus to please not let anything happen to my cat while I was gone.

I landed in Lima without incident and called my wife to let her know I was working my way home and hoped to be there late the following afternoon. I explained that Jesus told me to leave Peru, but I didn't know why. I caught a flight to Dallas and from there I was on my way home to San Diego. I knew something was wrong as soon as I saw my wife at the airport. She was holding a cat carrier. Instantly I surmised why Jesus had called me out of the jungle to come home so quickly. Apparently at the very moment my last flight left the ground from Dallas to San Diego, our cat Jen-a-fur had a stroke. She was still alive but not for much longer. My heart almost burst with joy when I realized that Jesus had brought me home in time to spend the last hours of Jenny's life with her.

What Jesus did for me was amazing. He sent me deep into the jungle with only one fear—that my beloved cat would die while I was gone. Then He orchestrated a series of miracles to get me home at exactly the right time so we could be together on her last day on earth. That is kindness and love beyond my comprehension. That is kindness and love that brings me to my knees in worship and adoration for the One who can show such love. I worship the One who has the power, grace and mercy to show His love to me in a way that strengthened my faith to extraordinary proportions. For that kindness and love I will be eternally grateful.

After that experience I knew that I could trust Jesus for anything and everything. Seeing Him miraculously paving the way before me, when it was otherwise humanly impossible, gave me extraordinary faith. I assumed that because I was obediently exercising the little amount of faith that He had initially given me, He was honoring that tiny bit of faith by doing miracles that dramatically increased my faith. It has now been many years where I have trusted Jesus and then watched His supernatural provision and miracles answer that trust. As a result, I have learned that extraordinary faith, or crazy faith as I have learned to call it, is something that Jesus is looking for. It is something I will be speaking about a lot in the pages following. For now, let me say that the more you have faith and trust in Jesus for the seemingly impossible, the more He delights in honoring your faith and doing miracles in answer to your prayers.

I want to speak about something important with regards to faith. In my experience faith has nothing at all to do with getting what you want. Faith is about trusting Jesus to accomplish in your life the things that *He* has asked you to do, not the things that you want to do. Not even ministry plans that you have dreamed up by yourself. If you listen, He will guide you. And what He has planned and declared for you to do, that is what He will accomplish through your faith in Him. Faith is beautiful and ever-growing. It allows you to say with conviction, "Jesus, I am obeying Your instructions and I now have a problem that only You can fix. I am declaring that I cannot fix this, and I am trusting You to fix it. It's Your problem now." I can't tell you how many times I have spoken those words to Jesus, but it has been a lot. Nor can I tell you how many times He has answered my prayers and done miraculous things, as I am sure He does many miracles that

I do not see happen and don't even know about. However, I can tell you that when I have obeyed His instructions, no matter how crazy they seemed at the time to myself and to others, I have never been disappointed in the outcome. Sure, some things didn't go as I planned, but exercising crazy faith in Jesus means that His plans will always be accomplished, and He can turn what the enemy means for evil into incredible goodness.

I think that sometimes Jesus takes us on a journey and then allows us to make mistake after mistake. Or he allows our enemy satan to harass us and get us into a lot of trouble. Then He reveals His protection over us as He rescues us out of dangerous or difficult situations that we cannot control. And I think He often does all that just to show us how much He loves us. What Jesus did for us on the cross was the most loving act in the history of the world. He didn't do it to impress anyone. He did it to rescue us, and I believe that above all else He simply wants us to know how much He loves us and how much He wants to spend eternity with us who love Him back.

Chapter 13

Casting Out Demons in India

It had been some time since returning from Peru, and the pain in my body was reaching new profound heights. Some days I literally crawled up the stairs to the bedroom. But still my crazy faith knew that Jesus had not kept me alive to sit home and whine about my infirmities. I prayed for information from Jesus about His plans, along with an open door, while others prayed for my healing.

Through her previous employer my wife was acquainted with the son of a well-known Christian leader of a large mission organization in India. John took teams of believers from the Los Angeles area to minister in India. They were trained in cultural protocols and had specific skills they could use and pass on to their Indian counterparts. Working in teams, they also went to schools and shared Jesus through music, drama, and puppet shows. From my wife John learned I was involved in sharing the gospel, so he invited me to go to India with him and his team. I was assigned to the puppet show team and went through their training and joined the mission trip to Chennai in southern India.

My health issues led to some concerns about going on this trip. The pain had become so severe that I could barely walk, yet I needed to help with the equipment and sets for our dramas and skits. On the drive to the airport, I was praising Jesus for giving me the opportunity to go to India and share His message of salvation with people who hadn't heard yet. Suddenly I felt what I can only describe as a switch being flipped in my brain. *All the pain that I had been feeling 24/7 for many years suddenly disappeared in an instant.* I was moved to tears and I praised Jesus for touching me and removing the pain.

The trip to India was amazing. However, after we did our show at the first school, I discovered something that gave me pause. Although we were singing songs about Jesus, and doing skits about Jesus, and performing puppet shows about Jesus, nobody clearly explained the gospel to the kids. Nor did anyone invite the large group of school kids to repent and accept and receive Jesus as Savior and Lord. The missed opportunity was disconcerting. As we traveled to the next school, I asked the leader of our group for permission to share the gospel at the next school. She was hesitant because they weren't accustomed to doing that, but I talked her into letting me do it.

At the next school there was a large crowd of kids in the auditorium. Once the different teams had finished with their performances I walked out onto the stage. I shared with them about Jesus using Scriptures from the Bible to explain repentance and salvation and asked them if they wanted to be saved. Almost every hand in the auditorium went up. A huge group of kids repented of their sins and prayed to accept and receive Jesus and be filled with the Holy Spirit.

The other members of the group were thrilled and excited to see so many responding positively to the gospel, but the group leader seemed to be upset with me. She asked me to not share the gospel at the next school. When I asked her the reason, she couldn't give me one. While I considered her request, there was no stopping me. When I saw a pause at the end of the program I rushed onto the stage and shared the gospel with the kids. We had traveled too far to not share the gospel with kids who didn't know about Jesus. If we didn't share the gospel, then what we were doing was merely providing entertainment, which is not what I or the others on the team had signed up for. There was no way I was going to pass up the opportunity to lead a bunch of kids to Christ.

My desire to evangelize caused some tension with the group leader. I knew that Jesus had commanded us in the Scriptures to share the gospel with every creature. I also knew that Jesus had saved me from death to specifically share the gospel with the unsaved. It would have taken more than her disfavor to get me to stop. I reasoned that I had been invited to India because I share the gospel openly and boldly, and until John, the mission leader, told me to stop, his opinion would trump hers. Amazingly, the Holy Spirit was present at each school we went to, and many kids chose to repent and believe the gospel of Jesus.

One afternoon our group drove out to a community outside the city for an evangelistic event. There was worship music at the outreach and a speaker who shared about Jesus and preached the gospel. Our group performed a drama skit. Prayer was offered at the end of the event and our group was invited to come forward to assist as there were many people wanting prayer. A young man approached me who was obviously very disturbed. He was anxious and fidgety, and his eyes were darting all over the place. Without a translator and with his limited English we tried to communicate. All I could understand was "demons." With no prior experience praying for someone to be delivered from demons, I laid one of my hands on his head, raised my other hand to heaven, and I prayed to Jesus for help. Then I ordered the demons in Jesus' name to leave the young man. I must confess that I was quite surprised when I felt a physical presence leave him. As I felt the presence leave, the young man's body immediately relaxed under my hand, and he stopped fidgeting. He looked up at me and his eyes were clear. He had the biggest smile on his face. "They left," he said as he began praising Jesus. So did I! It was an awesome thing to see Jesus working so powerfully from such a simple prayer.

Upon returning to San Diego, while driving home, I felt that same sensation of a switch being flipped in my brain. The pain that had miraculously vanished when leaving for India returned in full force. That was my first indication that perhaps Jesus did not want to heal me completely from my pain. It was to be several more years in His service before I came to fully understand why.

Chapter 14

Traveling Through Mexico

Not long after the trip to India a couple who ran the church's puppet ministry told me about an orphanage in Tecate, Mexico. Tecate was right across the border and only a couple hours from home. I visited the orphanage and met the wonderful Christian couple who ran it. The orphanage was in an old house, and it needed a lot of maintenance work, so I was blessed to be able to help with plumbing, electrical, carpentry, painting, etc. This also provided several opportunities to share the gospel with the kids and invite them to accept and receive Jesus as Savior and Lord.

When the 'to-do' list at the orphanage was finished I drove outside of Tecate to find other opportunities for ministry. On the road between Tecate and Tijuana I discovered pockets of very small communities living in tiny dwellings made from cardboard, sheets of plastic, cut up trash bags and the odd piece of plywood, over a framework of scrap wood and wooden poles. Most of the residents had little or no money, no work, and no hope for a better life. Many were women with kids, brought to Tecate from other parts of Mexico and left behind while their husbands crossed the border illegally into the USA looking for work. Of course the husbands would promise to return for their families, but for unknown reasons many never did. The women and kids were left stranded in these cardboard hovels.

There was a huge need for food, blankets, and warm clothing. I would frequently visit these areas with a pickup truck full of supplies to distribute. Driving into a cardboard community I put out the word that I had food, blankets, and clothing to give away. When a large crowd assembled around the truck I would stand up in the back of the pickup and share the gospel with everyone there and invite them to repent and accept and receive Jesus as Savior and Lord and trust Him alone for their salvation.

On subsequent visits to the same areas, I would share more from the Bible with the crowds. The gospel was well-received, and after many visits to one area in particular I felt like I was a part of their community.

In this community one of the old men built a small building from old poles and scrap lumber to use as a church. They held church services there and when I visited we would study and discuss the Bible and worship together. Everyone who came was encouraged to share what Jesus was saying to them. Or they might share a song or a teaching from the Bible. Someone was always prepared, and we had some wonderful times together in those meetings

It was common for one or two men from the Julian church to accompany me at times on these missions. Several times my wife came with me too. She was great with the kids. It was a great season of my life, ministering to and serving the poorest of the poor. It was an amazing journey as Jesus led us to specific people and places as we met their needs. It was an awesome Holy Spirit filled time of ministry.

It was interesting to me that Jesus almost always told me where and when He wanted me to go while I was sitting and reading the Bible. I would be reading Scripture and suddenly I would hear Him prompting, "Go to Mexico." I would immediately get up and make the arrangements to go.

As the Father Has Sent Me, I Also Send You

It was not long before I heard Jesus tell me to go to Central Mexico. I knew I had heard His voice clearly, but I didn't know anything about Central Mexico, so I got out the atlas and looked it up. Still, I wasn't sure exactly what the Lord's plan was for the trip, or where to go, so I was praying for clearer direction. One evening I was reading the book of Luke and the words seemed to reverberate right through me. I knew Jesus was speaking directly to me through His Word: *"The Spirit of the Lord is upon Me, Because He has anointed Me to preach the gospel to the poor; He has sent Me to heal the brokenhearted, To proclaim liberty to the captives and recovery of sight to the blind, To set at liberty those who are oppressed; To proclaim the acceptable year of the Lord."* [Luke 4:18]. Then immediately another Bible verse came to my mind in which Jesus said, *"As the Father has sent Me, I also send you."* [John 20:21].

I understood immediately that just as Jesus was sent to do those things, so He was sending me. This revelation confirmed the going and the doing. But where specifically was I supposed to go? I asked Jesus to tell me. Then I kept reading Luke 4. When I got to verse 43, I had my answer. "*...but He said to them, "I must preach the kingdom of God to the other cities also, because for this purpose I have been sent."* That was it. I had my instructions: Preach the gospel to the poor in all the towns and villages that I direct you to. It's for this purpose that He was sending me. In practical terms it meant I was to start driving and I would be told where to go as I travelled. I was ecstatic that He would speak so clearly to me through His Word.

Within a couple of days my good friend Troy volunteered to accompany me for about ten days. Then he would have to fly home because he had a full-time job and would have to go back to work. The elders of the church laid hands on us and prayed for us. Then we headed off to Mexico in my pickup truck with a camper shell on the back and a sign in the front windshield that Troy had made that read, *Souls for Heaven or Bust!*

The first day we drove until sundown, and we stayed overnight in a hotel in Santa Ana, Mexico. The next day we drove to Hermosillo where we picked up 2000 Spanish New Testaments from the Mexico Bible Society that were ordered before our departure. Bibles received and prayed over, Troy and I continued our drive. Suddenly we both felt that Jesus was leading us to stop at the next village.

Pulling into town we drove around looking for the town square. Pretty much every town and village in Mexico has a town square, most times directly in front of a Catholic church. We found and parked in front of the town square and set out with a cloth bag full of New Testaments and some balloons and a pump to make balloon animals. Troy's Spanish was not great, so he made balloon animals while I shared the gospel.

The first thing Troy made was an elaborate hat made from balloons with a balloon animal on the top. He put it on his head and within a minute or two several kids in the square saw him with his balloon hat and ran up to us excitedly. Troy made the kids a balloon animal or a balloon sword or a hat. With kids running around with their balloon gifts, word soon got out. Before long we had a group of kids and their parents gathered around us waiting their turn for one of Troy's balloon creations. When we had a decent sized group, Troy paused his balloon making while I shared the gospel and invited them all to get saved by Jesus.

In my travels I have found that using Scripture is always key to sharing the gospel. There is value in sharing your own testimony with unbelievers and to just talk about Jesus in familiar terms, and I will also do that, especially once they have heard the gospel. But in my experience, there is *nothing* that even comes close to touching people and opening their hearts and minds to Jesus than Bible verses about salvation. I have prepared a list of 14 Bible verses that speak specifically about salvation that is taped in the back of all my Bibles. The verses are in an order that clearly explains all aspects of the gospel to an unbeliever. Once all 14 verses are read to them, pausing in between each verse to ask and answer questions, I summarize what is required to be born again. Then I ask if they are ready to repent and turn from their sins and accept and receive Jesus as Savior and Lord and follow Him. You can find a copy of the Scriptures used to share the gospel in the Appendix at the end of the book titled: *"How to Share the Gospel."*

I have found that most of the people in Mexico are very humble and teachable, and eager to please God. But although most of the Mexicans I met are generally deeply religious and profess faith in the Catholic Church, nobody has told them what the Bible says about Jesus and salvation. It was rare and unusual for someone who listened to me share about Jesus to not repent and be saved. And for some, from the intensity with which they listened to the Scriptures and responded to the invitation to repent and trust Jesus for salvation, it was apparent this was something they had been needing to hear for a long time. Often at the moment of salvation, a visible release of joy and peace comes over them.

In that first town we met several Catholic priests on the street who were leaving the church at the end of the day. I asked them if they knew what the Bible said about Jesus and salvation. Only one of them stayed behind to talk to us while the others went their way. He spoke English, and both Troy and I shared Jesus with him for quite some time. At the end he did not repent or ask Jesus to save him. He said he was afraid that he would have to leave his position in the Catholic Church, since they saw the teaching of salvation through faith in Jesus alone as heretical. In Mexico, the Catholic Church teaches the people that to have any chance at all for salvation they must belong to the Catholic Church and adhere to all the Catholic traditions, rituals, and beliefs, many of which contradict clear teachings of the Bible.

Troy and I stopped and shared the gospel in several towns and villages before we continued south stopping in a village called San Juan Nuevo in the state of Michoacan. There we spent several days sharing the gospel on the streets and in the town square. We asked Jesus to help us find someone in the village who was already a believer. We were eager to find out if there were any groups of believers already meeting in the village as we wanted to have some place to send the new believers for discipling. After that prayer we walked aimlessly down the streets, continuing to pray, when we heard some singing coming from a house. We walked into the yard and a woman came outside. After speaking to her briefly the woman brought out the pastor who invited us inside. The group had heard there were gringos in town preaching the gospel but had not initially believed it. Their own experience as believers in this village was of being persecuted and threatened by the Catholic Church. They also told us that San Juan Nuevo is known for being a center for the occult and witchcraft.

We told them our story of traveling through Mexico sharing the gospel openly with all who came to the town square in each village. We told them that we had been doing it for several days in their village, and that so far, nobody had threatened us or tried to stop us. They were very encouraged by our experience and their faith was strengthened. As a group they determined to be bolder about sharing the gospel with others in town. I asked if they would like to join us going door-to-door in the village and telling people about Jesus. The pastor and one other man said they would like to come with us. The next day we went with them to share the gospel and several souls were added to the Kingdom of God.

Meeting Juan and Delia - True Servants of Jesus

We stayed in San Juan Nuevo several more days, sharing the gospel each day in the town square. Then it was time for Troy to fly home so we headed for the Guadalajara airport. After Troy left, I looked up an address in Guadalajara I had been referred to through a believer we met in one of the villages. When I knocked on the door I was warmly received and in just a few moments I realized that I had walked into a ministry that would warm my heart and fill me with joy. Heading the ministry was a brother named Juan and his wife Delia. There was an immediate connection with Juan, a joining of our hearts and spirits. We were both called from the depths of despair to serve Jesus and to take His message of salvation to the least and the lost. This shared commission united us together, and I understood instantly that the brother in front of me was going to be one of my very best friends to the end of my life. At that first meeting we were knit together by Jesus into an unbreakable bond of friendship.

Over the next few days we prayed, laughed, and wept together. We shared our life stories with each other and how Jesus had saved us and called us to share His message of salvation with others. Juan had been a heroin addict for many years. Before he met Jesus, he had lived a gang life of crime, and had spent 10 years in federal prison in the USA for a murder conviction. That's where he met Jesus. After prison he returned to Mexico where he started a street ministry directed at drug addicts.

The house had two stories but was only about 1500 square feet in total. Yet there were fifteen men living there along with Juan and his wife. There were two bathrooms in the house for seventeen people. All fifteen men were ex-alcoholics and drug addicts. During the day Juan and Delia ministered to the men, conducting Bible studies and group meetings. In the evenings they had a worship service.

Meeting them was an incredible experience for me. Juan was so in love with Jesus, and he and his wife Delia poured their lives out daily for these recovering addicts. The worship times in the evening were amazing and uplifting. The first evening Juan asked if I would lead them in prayer. Someone turned down the lights and as soon as I started to pray, everyone joined in simultaneously. I had never experienced prayer like this in America, everyone praying at the same time was incredible and I loved it. The emotion and worship that came out in the prayers was very touching. Grown men fell to their knees and wept in thanksgiving for their salvation. It was extremely healing and uplifting. Then someone picked up a guitar and started to sing a worship song. He didn't get through one verse before everyone in the room began singing their own song to Jesus. Although we were all singing different songs in the Spirit, our hearts were united in worship with Him. And it was all somehow harmonious and connected, as if angels were turning our individual songs into a choir. I wept tears of joy through it all.

Chapter 15

Bandits on the Highway

On my way home from Central Mexico I would stop in the small towns and villages along the way and repeat what Troy and I had been doing, but it was not the same as it had been with Troy. I then understood why Jesus sent His followers out two by two. Having someone to pray and minister with is so much more encouraging and enriching than doing it on your own.

As I made my way towards home, the long road heading north for the border was almost deserted. Only very occasionally would a car pass by going in the opposite direction. Seemingly out of nowhere I came upon five men standing in the middle of the road. They had several vehicles blocking the highway and were holding assault weapons. They motioned for me to stop. Having no other option, I stopped. I knew I was about to be robbed.

One of the men motioned for me to drive off the highway and down a small dirt road that was at a right angle to the highway. I could see that the road was leading into an area with natural rock walls on both sides and hidden from the highway. I then realized that I was not only going to be robbed, I was also very likely going to be killed and my truck stolen. My pickup truck was almost brand new, so I knew there was no way I was going to be keeping it. I also knew that they were not going to leave a witness.

I had perfect peace. I knew this had to be the will of God, or I would not be in this predicament. There was a real sense of comfort that passed over me, blocking any opportunity for fear to enter. I felt that peace that the Bible speaks of, peace that passes all understanding. I was so happy that I was going to be seeing Jesus shortly.

I drove down the side road very slowly, keeping pace with one of the men who was walking beside the truck with his assault weapon leveled at me. Speaking to Jesus I said, "This is it. I'll be seeing You in a few minutes." The man walking beside the truck shouted at me to stop. Then he stepped closer to the driver's door pointing his gun in my face. He asked me, "Where are the drugs and the money?" I guess they figured that a lone gringo in a new pickup truck was in Mexico to buy drugs. I imagined that they assumed that I had drugs well hidden in the truck to get through customs. Clearly it would be easier for them to get me to tell them where the drugs were than to have to strip down the truck to find them.

I told him that I didn't have any drugs and that I had very little money. I told him that I had some New Testaments and that I was traveling through Mexico sharing about Jesus with the people. I asked him if he knew what the Bible said about Jesus and salvation. He looked at me angrily and made stabbing gestures with his rifle and said much louder this time, "Where are the drugs and the money?"

I repeated what I had already told him, visibly frustrating him. He swore at me and stormed off. A couple minutes later a very large man walked up to the driver's door. He pointed his assault weapon at me demanding, "Tell me right now where the drugs and the money are!" I repeated that I didn't have any drugs and had very little money. It was all too obvious that once the thieves recognized I would not share useful information, they would force me out of the truck, and I would be shot. Determined to share with him about Jesus before he shot me, I knew that I needed to keep talking. I said the first thing that came into my mind.

"What kind of gun is that?" I asked. He looked at me bewildered that I would ask such a question, and he replied while shaking his head, "It's an AK-47." I told him that it was a very nice gun. Then I asked him, "Do you want to see my weapon?" He looked at me shocked that I would say such a thing at such a time as this. I think at this point he thought I was crazy or that I had seriously misunderstood my situation. His response was unintelligible to me—a cross between bewilderment and cursing. He thrust his AK-47 closer to my face.

I repeated, "Would you like to see my weapon?" He strained to look past me through the open window to see if he could see a weapon in the truck. I told him that my weapon was not like his as I slowly reached with my right hand and picked up a Spanish New Testament off the seat next to me. I held it up and said, "This is my weapon, the Word of God, the sword of the Spirit."

The man looked at me in disbelief, and I could see that he was confused and conflicted. He truly did not know what to do. He turned around and looked at the other men that were in sight. He stared at them for what seemed like a long time. Then he turned back and looked at me, seemingly lost in thought and indecision. Finally, he reached into the right front pocket of his cargo pants and held up a small leather bound Spanish New Testament. He looked me right in the eyes, locking his eyes on mine, and he said, "I also have the sword of the Spirit, and YOU (he really emphasized the YOU) are free to go." Then he gestured for me to turn around and drive back to the highway. I turned around and drove slowly down the side road. I had to drive past the other armed men whose faces showed shock and confusion as I drove by. They were staring back at the big guy gesturing as to what they should do. He waved at them to let me go. And off I went with my faith strengthened and my heart encouraged.

Chapter 16

Back to San Juan Nuevo

At the direct prompting of Jesus, I made three more trips by airline to Guadalajara and on to San Juan Nuevo over the next six months, sharing the gospel in the town square and on the streets. This was at a time when the ankylosing spondylitis was causing such inflammation and degeneration of my soft tissue that I was in unbearable pain 24/7, and now almost paralyzed from the pain in my hips and spine. At times the pain was so intense that I would get up from a chair to walk across the room and I couldn't do it. Just the act of standing up caused so much pain that my brain would shut off the connection to my hips, spine, and legs, leaving me unable to even move. Standing in place temporarily paralyzed was so absurd that I would start to laugh. It was both comical and pathetic. Yet I was committed to obeying Jesus and going anywhere and doing anything He asked of me, so I knew that somehow I would just have to deal with the unrelenting pain.

One day while on the porch reading the Bible, I again heard Jesus telling me to return to San Juan Nuevo. But this time I was confused since I could barely walk from the living room to the kitchen. So instead of getting up and booking my flight like I normally would have done, I hesitated. "Lord, how am I going to do this? I can barely walk and there is no way I can carry even a small piece of luggage, let alone a box of New Testaments. How am I going to fly down there and function?" I did not receive a reply.

Over the next two weeks I frequently heard Jesus ask me, "Are you going back to San Juan Nuevo?" Each time I answered that I desired to go, but I couldn't physically obey. The Lord's persistence and my now familiar repetitive replies became almost amusing. "Jesus, all You would have to do is touch me. Just one little touch from You and I will be healed enough to go." But despite my pleadings, there was no reply and no healing.

When He asked me yet again if I was going to go back to San Juan Nuevo, I became so frustrated that I simply replied, "Okay, You win. I am going to San Juan Nuevo as You've asked, but I have no idea how I am going to manage it. I guess that's Your problem now Lord." I immediately booked my flight.

The very next morning I was awoken by a knock on the door. Struggling to get out of bed and down the stairs, I opened the door and greeted my friend Elmo. He told me that the night before, as he was praying, Jesus asked him to come with me to San Juan Nuevo to carry my luggage and Bibles. I started to weep with joy when I understood that when Jesus asked me to go, He knew that I was not physically capable of obeying Him. He wanted to see if I was willing to obey Him and go anyway. And once I decided that I would just obey Him without reservation, that was when He supplied the help I needed.

Faith Breeds Possibilities

The trip to San Juan Nuevo with Elmo was a wonderfully spiritual trip. Where I might at times forget to pray, Elmo is a brother who is always praying. He is truly what they call a prayer warrior. Elmo has a very humble soul and a huge heart; he is the proverbial servant Christian, with no ego and no job is too small or demeaning for him. Although Elmo could only speak a few words and phrases in Spanish, he was happy and content to come along to carry my luggage and Bibles. I was humbled by his willingness to obey Jesus and journey alongside me.

However, it soon became clear that there would also be some spiritual warfare accompanying us on this mission trip. When we arrived, there was a huge crowd at the airport in Tijuana due to an airline pilot strike in process. All the flights out of Tijuana on the airline I had booked had been cancelled for the foreseeable future.

We started to pray. While we prayed, we tried to find flights with another airline. I asked at the counter if they had two seats on the next flight to Guadalajara. The guy looked at me like I was crazy (nothing new to me). He said with a very annoyed tone, "Look around you man. Look at all these people. Does it look like we would have two seats on the next flight to Guadalajara? Every flight for days is sold out." I knew that Jesus had told me to go on this trip, and that He had told Elmo to come with me. I also had faith that Jesus could do anything, so I asked him again, "Are you *sure* that you don't have two seats available on the next flight to Guadalajara? Could you please just check for me."

He looked at me with bewildered contempt and anger that I would ask him such a stupid thing in such an obviously impossible situation. To get me to go away he started punching keys on his computer keyboard. Suddenly his face changed from anger to total confusion. He looked at me with a shocked expression, then looked back at his computer screen incredulously. Then he leaned over the counter and said to me quietly, "I'm not sure how or why this is possible. A lot of people here have been trying to get seats on this same flight, and the flight has been completely sold out. But my computer is showing that there are two seats available on the next flight to Guadalajara leaving in a few minutes. Would you like them?" I flashed him a very big smile, and in a short time Elmo and I were in the air on our way to Guadalajara. We were praising Jesus as we went. How amazing that Jesus was able to miraculously get us on that sold-out flight.

After that experience we were encouraged to pray even more. Leaving nothing to chance, we prayed about everything during that trip. We lifted all our plans and needs up to Jesus. Since He asked us to make the trip, we trusted Him to work out all the details.

We hired a taxi to take us all the way from the airport in Guadalajara to San Juan Nuevo. Along the way the taxi was stopped by several armed men. They were in some type of uniform, but they were bedraggled and unkept, so my first thought was that they were bandits. Assuming we were about to be robbed, I started to pray. I knew that Elmo would be praying too. One of the men asked us to get out of the car. "No," I said, "we are not getting out of the car." This time he shouted while waving his gun. "Get out of the car!" "No," I repeated, "that's not going to happen. We are here to serve Jesus and we will not get out of the car." He didn't know what to do so he cursed at me and turned away to talk to his buddies. Taking advantage of the opportunity, the taxi driver quickly sped off. We looked at each other in amazement knowing that Jesus was truly in control, and He would save us from any harm that the enemy intended for us.

By now I was well known in the village. People would greet me in the hotel and the markets and on the streets. We rented the same room that I always stayed in, and the next morning we headed for the town square to preach the gospel. Elmo had learned how to make balloon animals, so we did the same thing I had done with Troy. Elmo would make balloons to attract a crowd and then I would share the gospel when we had a good-sized group together.

During our second day of ministry a young man approached me. He told me that the priest in the Catholic Church was telling the people during the services that there were some gringos in the town square telling lies to the people. He warned them to not listen to us. The young man advised us to leave town as they might do something to stop us. I thanked him for telling me. Then I explained that Jesus had sent us there to share His message of salvation with the people, and that was what we were going to do. I asked if I could share the gospel with him, but he was too afraid of being seen with us.

The following day as we were leaving the town square, an old man walked up to me and tightly grabbed my arm. He got intimidatingly close to my face and told me that he was with the Catholic Church. He spoke angrily and said that I was not welcome in their town and that I was to leave right away and never come back. I said to him, "I am very sorry, but I am not able to do as you say. Jesus asked me to come here to speak to the people and I must obey Him." He looked at me like I was crazy, not knowing of course that I was, crazy for Jesus. "You take your book and go home," he said, "and if you come back tomorrow, we will beat you badly." I thanked him for the warning and repeated that we could not comply. He shook his head and walked away.

At the town square the next morning, while sharing the gospel with a woman, I looked up and spotted the same old man with a younger man standing beside him. They were both holding long round sticks about 3 inches in diameter, staring at me with murder in their eyes. The old man walked over to me and forced himself onto the bench between myself and the woman. The woman immediately left, and the old man said angrily to me, "I told you not to come back here, and now we are going to beat you. I will give you one last chance. Take your evil book and leave town right now and we won't beat you." I asked him, "Why do you say my book is evil? It is the Bible, the Word of God!" He said, "Just take your book and go."

I know enough about Mexico to use a Catholic Bible when I share the gospel there. That way I can't be accused of using a mistranslated version. Though the Catholic Old Testament has added some books that are not included in any other Bibles, the Catholic New Testament has the same content as other translations. I challenged the old man to look at my book, showing him the inside front page of the Bible where it said it was copyrighted by the Catholic Bible Society in Rome and authorized by the Pope. He was speechless. I then asked him, "Will you please do me a favor?" He said, "No! We didn't come here to do you a favor. We came to beat you and make you leave our town." I added, "Yes, I know that you came here to beat me. But will you please let me read to you exactly what I have been reading to the other people here? Then you can tell me if you think it is wrong. After you hear what I have been telling the people, if you still want to beat me, no problem." He was both confused and intrigued, so he just nodded and said, "Okay."

I began with Romans 1:16 and continued to share several verses with him. His angry face softened with each Scripture. I could see that the words I was speaking to him from the Bible were touching his heart. After sharing more Scriptures, at an appropriate moment I asked him, "Are you ready to repent of your sins and open your heart to Jesus Christ and ask Him to save you?" With tears in his eyes he replied, "Yes, I am ready." When his young friend who was still standing about fifteen feet away holding onto his stick saw the old man tearing up and bowing his head to pray, he quickly left. As for the old man, the stick he was still holding in his hand was forgotten and right there he gave his life to Jesus. At that moment I fully understood the meaning of the Scripture in Hebrews 4:12 that reads: *"The Word of God is living and powerful, and sharper than a two-edged sword, piercing even to the division of soul and spirit, and of the joints and marrow, and is a discerner of the thoughts and intents of the heart."* In that moment I visualized a large sword coming down on that old man's head and splitting him in two, as the Holy Spirit convicted him of sin, and his mind and heart bowed in repentance to Jesus.

After we had prayed and I had shared some more Scriptures with the old man, he asked me if I would come to his house and teach him more about Jesus and the Bible. Of course I agreed, and went to tell Elmo who had been busy making balloons for the kids in the park.

I told Elmo that the old man had just been saved and wants us to now visit his home and teach him more about Jesus. Elmo was not comfortable about leaving with the old man. He reminded me that the old man had come with a younger man with sticks to beat me, who was probably waiting somewhere for the old man to bring us to a non-public place to beat us. Because I had witnessed the old man's response to the Word of God, I assured Elmo that it wasn't a trap; he genuinely was seeking more Scripture.

We arrived at a large blue gate, and the property was completely enclosed by a high blue corrugated metal fence. We went into a yard on the side of the house, and the old man brought out some chairs and there we sat and had an hour-long Bible study together. About 15 minutes into our study, I recognized a young man walking through the yard on his way out. As he went out the gate I asked the old man, "Who is that?" "That's my grandson," he replied. Rejoicing, I reported that his grandson had prayed with me in the town square the day before and had received Jesus as Savior and Lord. He was very thankful to hear that.

Elmo and I also attended the small house church in San Juan Nuevo. The pastor's message was on repentance. He was such a wonderful example of humility as he wept before his congregation and asked their forgiveness if he had ever offended any of them. The pastor spoke of the equality of all believers, and he gave an incredible object lesson on how each person in the congregation was as important to the body of Christ as he was. There was much weeping and repentance that night.

Since my last visit the congregation had decided that it was time to become public and they had been searching for a small piece of land to build a church. They had looked at several properties and decided as a congregation to purchase a specific parcel of land. The members of the congregation are all very poor. They were trying to complete the purchase of the land, but they still needed $500 more to complete the purchase. I quickly asked Jesus what to do and I got an immediate confirmation in my spirit that I should provide the additional money needed. A couple days later the purchase was completed, and Elmo and I were blessed to witness the small congregation dedicate their new church property to the Lord in prayer. What wonderful timing that the Lord had us there for the privilege of sharing that moment with them.

The presence of God and the power of the Holy Spirit was so evident on that trip with Elmo. Each morning and evening we would worship the Lord together in our hotel room and pray together. The Lord was so close to us, and it was incredible. Before leaving on the trip, I had been praying for boldness and I also asked others to pray for that as well. The prayers were answered as the gospel went out with a boldness that could only have come from the Lord through the Holy Spirit. Hearts were touched and changed right before our eyes. We rejoiced in what a privilege it was to serve such a loving God.

Chapter 17

Being Prepared by God - The Hard Way

My health took a turn for the better in the year 2000 when a new drug "Vioxx" came onto the market. It was primarily indicated to treat rheumatoid arthritis, but it was also purported to help people like me who were suffering with ankylosing spondylitis (AS). I once had a doctor tell me that AS was similar to rheumatoid arthritis, but instead of the pain being only in your joints, it is in all the soft tissue of your body. For me, that included all the muscles and ligaments throughout my body. It even affects my teeth and my eyes. I have experienced incredible pain in almost every part of my body. After the first couple of months on Vioxx there was no improvement in the pain. I was tempted to quit taking it since it was also known that it didn't work for everyone. I was asking Jesus to heal me or to make the medication work, so I kept taking it.

And one day the Vioxx suddenly started to work, and the relief was very noticeable. The pain was not gone, but it was reduced to a point where I no longer needed two canes to go upstairs. I could now get around again and carry my own luggage when the Lord sent me out. I was so thankful to the Lord for having even this moderate relief.

Crohn's Disease

After battling the pain of ankylosing spondylitis for decades, I didn't think my health could get any worse, but in 2001 it did. I was under a lot of stress at the time. In addition to the ministry work, I was employed as a real estate agent, while also starting up a new online business to pay our bills. It hit so suddenly that the precise moment is still clear in my memory. I was in the real estate office when suddenly the stress I was under exploded in my stomach. I immediately felt a burning sensation that spread from my stomach to my intestines. It was very painful and over the next couple of weeks worsened. I was bleeding internally, and when it felt as if I was dying, I ended up in the hospital emergency room. The doctor discovered that I had lost so much blood that I was severely dehydrated. They put me on an IV drip for several hours and I recovered somewhat.

A local doctor examined me and ran some tests a few days later. I had already researched my symptoms online and suspected that I had Crohn's disease. The doctor who had diagnosed me with AS years before told me that there were two "sister diseases" that accompany AS in people carrying the genetic marker HLAB27 antigen. They are Reiter's Syndrome, which is what I had when I was diagnosed with AS, and Crohn's disease, which was obviously manifesting in my body now.

My local doctor referred me to a specialist in San Diego, who confirmed that I had this disease, and for the following 20 years I struggled with severe Crohn's symptoms. Over the years I tried an assortment of toxic Crohn's drugs, special supplements, restrictive diets, etc., none of which kept me free from serious Crohn's symptoms for longer than a month or two. However, neither AS nor Crohn's disease ever stopped me from serving Jesus and going wherever He told me to go. His love and grace have always been sufficient to carry me through.

Chapter 18

Called to Afghanistan

Getting up one morning in the Spring of 2003, I felt a sudden and distinct burden in my heart for Afghanistan. I found that very curious since I knew nothing about Afghanistan. I had not thought much about that country other than a quick prayer for peace now and again when I was prompted by something in the news.

My curiosity led me to get out our atlas. Seeing where Afghanistan was located, I looked up and said, "Jesus, why did You suddenly give me a burden for Afghanistan?" His reply was, "Go and see!"

I commenced my research. How to get there? How to get a visa? How long should I plan on staying? What accommodations will be available? Who to contact while I'm there? I was able to find answers to the first three questions rather quickly, and my research on places to stay gave me the name of a hotel in Kabul. That left tackling the mystery of what to do in Afghanistan. I contacted as many Christian Organizations as I could to ask if they were serving inside Afghanistan. I was not successful in finding anyone in the USA who had been to that country. Eventually I did find the name of two organizations and the names of a missionary couple serving there. I contacted them all by email, and I got their phone numbers to call them when I got to Kabul. About three months after I got the call from Jesus to go to Afghanistan, I arrived in Kabul.

Into the Darkness

Kabul was a dark and depressing city. For the entire time I was there it was as if there was a heavy weight pulling me down. It was difficult to pray, and the spiritual oppression was palpable. Crohn's symptoms added a physical element to this oppression, and since I could not speak the language, I wasn't able to effectively communicate with anyone.

My ten-day trip went by slowly. I only had three contacts and I made appointments with all three as soon as I arrived. While waiting for the meetings I had nothing to do except walk the streets to pray and view the sights. Communication with the locals was restricted to mostly hand and facial gestures.

My first meeting was with the head of one of the Christian organizations working in Kabul. The meeting was extremely unnerving and distressing. I met the gentleman at his office and asked what his organization was doing in Afghanistan. He told me about the projects they were involved in. There was no mention of the gospel or any spiritual activities. I inquired about that and was told it was not possible to share the gospel in Afghanistan, such activity was far too dangerous. He also said they could not distribute Christian literature or Bibles to the people as they are banned in Afghanistan.

My face no doubt relayed my shock. His reply to my asking what they were doing as Christians in Afghanistan was, "We are sharing the love of Jesus with the people." This response caught me off guard. And being entirely undiplomatic and without filters, I blurted out, "If you never tell them about Jesus and how to get saved, but you just show them the love of Jesus, does that mean that when they die and go to hell, they will be thinking that you Christians are nice people? What good does that do them?"

Obviously offended, he asked me, "Why did you come to Afghanistan?" I replied, "I don't know yet, but Jesus called me to preach the gospel, so I assume that when he called me to Afghanistan it was to preach the gospel here." My words rankled him, and he immediately stood up and told me that I was a dangerous man. He said he would appreciate it if I didn't mention his name or his organization's name to anyone ever. He also said that I should never contact him again. I was shocked at his response and said so. He said that since I was planning to talk to people in Afghanistan about Jesus, I was essentially his enemy. He also said that my actions would make it dangerous for him and other Christians to be in Afghanistan. He insisted that I leave his office immediately. I left his office shaking my head and trying to figure out what had just happened.

Next, I met with one of the leaders of another Christian organization. He came to my hotel for the meeting. Although not as rude to me as the first guy, he was very clear that it was not possible to share the gospel in Afghanistan and he didn't want to be involved in such activities. A few days later I met with the missionary couple I had contacted. They were teaching at a small school where the foreign missionaries sent their kids. I wanted to find out as much as I could, so I refrained from discussing why I was called to come to Afghanistan. Instead, I focused on encouraging them to talk specifically about what they were doing in Afghanistan.

They also shared that they were in Afghanistan to show the love of Jesus to the people. I asked them what they were doing to share the gospel with Afghans. They told me that the accepted protocol among the missionaries was that you should never talk to an Afghan about Jesus until you have known them for three to seven years. Even then you should only answer their specific questions. They said the goal was to pray and hope that eventually they would ask enough questions to understand the gospel. Just like the first two NGO leaders, it was clear that sharing the gospel was not the goal of these Christians either. Speaking about Jesus and sharing the gospel with Afghans would put them and all the other foreign missionaries in jeopardy, or so I was told. I left that meeting more confused than ever. To see such fear and negativity in sharing the gospel was heartbreaking to me. I wondered why Jesus had asked me to "go and see" this heartbreaking situation.

Preparing for the Battle

After returning home I asked Jesus about my journey, "Lord, that was a very depressing trip, and I am very confused. Why in the world did You send me there?" His reply was, "I wanted you to see the situation in Afghanistan. And now I want you to figure out how to share the gospel openly there. When you have learned how, then I want you to teach others how to do the same." Well at least I knew why He had burdened me for Afghanistan. But I had no idea how I was going to accomplish what He had asked me to do. I felt overwhelmed and out of my league.

The next four years were spent learning the Dari language, studying the social culture, and researching Afghanistan and Islam. In addition to language study, I also sought out and read every book that I could get my hands on that spoke at all about witnessing to Muslims. I sought out books written by missionaries who had served in Muslim countries, and books teaching methods for sharing the gospel with Muslims. Most of the books had the same theme: Islam is a false religion, Muhammad is a false prophet, and the Qur'an was inspired by a demon. They presented facts and information that sought to prove these assertions. Eventually I knew more about Islam and Muhammad than most Muslims knew. However, like most Muslims, I had not read the Qur'an.

During that period of preparation, I also attended a conference sponsored by people who were working in Afghanistan. There I met missionaries and representatives from various Christian Non-Profit Organizations that were serving in Afghanistan. It was great to meet so many missionaries who were either serving in Afghanistan or preparing to go there. Sadly I learned that the primary missionary model promoted at the conference was the same as what the two organization leaders and the two missionaries told me previously in Kabul. The general belief was that the gospel could not be preached openly in Afghanistan. The missionaries were going there to show the love of Christ to the Afghans through various medical and social programs. They hoped Afghanistan would eventually become more open to the gospel. Since Jesus had been clear that my mission was to learn how to share the gospel openly in Afghanistan, and to train others to do the same, I eagerly waited for His call for me to go back again.

Returning to Afghanistan

By 2007 I had enough language skills for basic conversation and could read Arabic script. Jesus said it was time to return. Since I was not being sent out by any ministry or organization, I would be entering Afghanistan on a tourist visa which was limited to three months. My goal was to quickly find an Afghan to teach me more of the language. I planned to study the language several hours every day until I was fluent enough to share the gospel in Dari.

I rented a room at the guest house of one of the Christian NGO's working in Kabul. Living in Kabul demanded a big adjustment from my American lifestyle. Electricity was available only once every two or three days, and then for a couple of hours at most, and running water was a luxury for only a few hours most days.

At the guest house I met two ladies from Australia who were missionaries to Afghanistan and had been serving as nurses for several years. We were the only long-term occupants of the house at that time. We talked a lot, sharing our stories and callings. But they struggled to understand what I was doing in Afghanistan. They couldn't understand how I had come to Afghanistan without being sent by an established NGO, since it was their understanding that everyone had to be associated with a supporting ministry.

I explained that I had a three-month tourist visa and planned to share the gospel with Afghans and discover how to do that openly without being arrested or killed. They were astounded that someone would even attempt to share the gospel in Afghanistan. Their organization leaders had trained them that it was too dangerous to talk about Jesus in that country.

They finally determined that I must be crazy. I assured them that "crazy" was probably the most accurate word they could use to describe me. They told the couple that were overseeing the house what I was doing. The director of the organization was out of the country, but the leader left in charge was curious and interested enough to invite me to a couple of their weekly meetings. It was very gracious of him to include me, and they were all very warm and sociable people, and I enjoyed their company.

The two Australians introduced me to an Afghan woman giving language lessons to people in their organization. Samira was willing to teach me, so I studied with her four days a week for several hours. We spent most of the study sessions talking in Dari about many things. As with all the Afghans I met, Samira was a Muslim. I was focused on sharing the gospel with her, so during our classes I told her all about Jesus and the Bible and I explained to her the Good News of salvation through faith in Jesus. Samira in turn shared about Islam and what she believed. My extensive research into Islam and Muhammad equipped me to argue some critical points on why Islam is a false religion and Muhammad is not a true prophet of God.

Not surprisingly, such discussion was not well received, and Samira was quite offended by my criticism of Islam and Muhammed. I reasoned that I was justified in speaking against Islam as I was telling her the truth. But it quickly became clear that my words were closing her mind and heart to the gospel. So instead, I focused more on sharing the gospel with her, rather than discussing the negative aspects of Islam. However, at times she would ask me questions that led back to me explaining some negative element within Islam. But when I did that, everything worked against the process and decreased her willingness to listen to the gospel.

During the sessions we also talked about our lives, our families, and our experiences. Samira had a fiancé who was a strong Muslim. Although interested in, and at times touched and moved by the gospel message, Samira resisted, because to become a Christian meant losing her future husband. It was also highly likely she would lose her entire family and all her friends as well. She mentioned that becoming a Christian would put her life in danger. My talks with Samira taught me how challenging evangelizing in Afghanistan would be. Samira left Kabul shortly thereafter to get married, and a young man named Amir became my language tutor.

Studying with Amir

Since I had learned a great deal about Islam from Samira, I was better able to discuss the differences between Islam and Christianity with Amir. I only shared with him the negative things about Islam when his religion came up in conversation naturally, but I spent much more time sharing the gospel with him. Yet I noticed the same thing happening with Amir as with Samira. Regardless of how I approached the subject, when I spoke negatively about Islam and Muhammad, he pulled back and was much less open to the gospel message.

As the time neared for me to return home, Amir very cautiously shared that he believed what I had been saying about Jesus. He didn't want to come right out and say it, as he was very fearful, but he hinted enough that I knew he was trying to tell me that he was a secret believer in Jesus. I embraced him and encouraged him, and for the rest of our classes I spent our time making sure that he clearly understood the message of the gospel. Initially he was confused about a lot of things regarding the gospel. However,

I made certain that he was secure in his salvation by the time I left Afghanistan.

My instruction from Jesus was to find a way to share the gospel openly in Afghanistan, but my current approach was not particularly successful. From experience I now knew that pointing out the negative aspects of Islam offended both of my language teachers, which alienated them and interfered with their openness. I concluded that this method of sharing the gospel with Muslims would likely result in persecution, arrest, or death, especially if done in the wrong situation or with the wrong people. I now understood why the Christian leaders said the gospel could not be shared in Afghanistan. No wonder many were afraid to even say the name of Jesus there.

Because arguing against Islam and the Qur'an was so offensive, the gospel would never be preached openly in Afghanistan using such a direct approach. I couldn't see how to avoid offending Muslims if there was to be a genuine and honest exchange about the problematic elements of Islam, Muhammad, and the Qur'an, which comprised the entire cornerstone for the Afghan worldview. But Jesus had asked me to share the gospel openly, so I continued praying and asking Jesus to help me figure it all out.

I actively sought out Afghan believers through the missionaries I met. Most of them didn't know of any. Occasionally I would meet someone who knew an Afghan, or had heard of one perhaps, who was a Christian. Finally, I managed to meet several Afghan men who claimed to be Christians. I quickly found out that they too were afraid to speak with anyone about Jesus, or even to say His name to anyone but another Christian.

I was further shocked to hear that most of them had never even shared about Jesus with their wives or kids. When I asked them why, they said that the foreign missionaries had told them that it would be too dangerous to tell *anyone* that they had become Christians. They were also warned that if they told their wife, and their wife told her father, they could be persecuted. And if they told their kids, the kids might inadvertently say something at school that could bring persecution on the family.

I discovered that none of them had a clear understanding of Jesus and salvation. Undoubtedly this deficiency was because most of the Christian organizations had adopted the protocol of never clearly sharing the full gospel with the Afghans. By restricting themselves to just answering questions from Afghans about Jesus when they came up, there was no way for the Afghans to ever fully grasp the message of the gospel. Although some claimed they had "changed their religion" most of them had not been saved. I realized I was facing a far bigger problem than I had expected.

I could see that most of the missionaries I spoke with desired to share the gospel with the Afghans. I understood why they were so fearful, and I wanted to speak to that fear. I would discuss that as the body of Christ working as missionaries in Afghanistan, if we were obeying Jesus and preaching the gospel openly, we should expect that some of us each year would be martyred for evangelizing. I reminded them that ten of the twelve disciples who walked with Jesus were martyred for sharing their faith. In the early church, martyrdom was considered normal and could be expected as Christians obeyed the command of Jesus to *"Go into all the world and share the gospel with every creature."* [Mark 16:15]. I also reminded them that the Bible is clear that we are to lay down our lives to get the gospel to the lost. And laying down our lives means that some of us will lose our lives. The good news is that we get to go to heaven when that happens.

I could see that some of the missionaries were excited and encouraged by the ideas I was sharing with them. They were bold and fearless warriors of Christ by even bringing themselves and their families into such a dangerous environment. But more was required than just to prepare these saints for persecution or death for sharing the gospel. That is not what Jesus had asked me to do. These missionaries and Afghan Christians needed better tools to share the gospel, especially since so much fear had penetrated their hearts and minds. It would be crucial for me to follow Jesus' instructions to find a method for sharing the gospel openly with Muslims, one that would be welcomed by the Muslims. It would be crucial for both my sake and for the sake of the missionaries serving there, as well as the Afghan believers. I knew that was a near impossible task. But since Jesus had asked me to do it, I figured that He would open the doors needed to accomplish it.

Chapter 19

Finding the Bridge

During my stay at the guest house in Kabul I met a lady from another country who came by one day to visit another guest. Her English, though not perfect, was good enough for us to communicate. I learned that she and her husband were missionaries sent from a church in their home country to Afghanistan. We talked extensively and I realized that like me they were also crazy for Jesus. She told me that she and her husband had been sent to Afghanistan by Jesus for the same reason I had been sent, which was to share the gospel and to find Afghan believers whom they could train to share the gospel.

They had started both a business and a language school. The husband was running the business, and she was running the language school. They were teaching English which is very popular with most young people in Afghanistan. She asked me if I was interested in teaching English to the kids. I told her that I only had a couple of weeks left in Afghanistan but would be happy to come several days a week to teach the kids English and tell them more about Jesus.

One day when I came to teach, she handed me a book that she had received at a recent seminar and was offering to lend it to me. Not only did I read the book, I devoured it. It was the breakthrough I had been praying for.

The basic message of the book was that there was a verse in the Qur'an that could be used to get Muslims interested in the gospel. I had read everything I could find on Islam and Muhammad and how to share the gospel with Muslims, but in all my research I never encountered the information presented in this book. Since I was soon returning to the USA, and because I didn't have a Qur'an in English, I didn't have a chance to try out this new information before leaving Afghanistan.

As soon as I returned home, I bought a Qur'an in English and read it through from beginning to end. I was surprised at how many times I read the name of Jesus in the Qur'an, as well as the names of some of the Old Testament prophets. There were also multiple references to "the previous books"—a reference to the Old and New Testament of the Bible.

Then I read through the Qur'an a second time, this time highlighting all mentions of Jesus and any references to quotes from the Bible or stories related to the Bible. I found that about 40% of the Qur'an referred to or retold Biblical accounts, especially from Old Testament passages. However, many of the details in the Qur'an directly conflicted with the same stories in the Bible. Upon further research to determine the reason for these discrepancies I learned that Muhammad was illiterate; he could not read the Bible himself and his compilations were based on oral retellings of the Biblical passages from obviously unreliable sources.

Selecting verses that appeared most helpful when using the Qur'an to start a conversation with Muslims about Jesus and the Bible, it was surprising to discover that many basics of Christianity are also found in the Qur'an, such as:

- Jesus is called the Word of God.
- Jesus is the Messiah and He was born of a virgin.
- Jesus healed the blind, and people with leprosy, and He raised the dead.
- Jesus is the right path, and the straight path, and Muslims are instructed to follow Jesus.

- God caused Jesus to die and then raised Him from the dead.

- When Jesus returns, His followers will go with Him where He is going, and those who do not follow and obey Jesus will suffer punishment in this world and in the hereafter, and there will be no one to help them.

- Muhammad did not have a new message, rather he came to confirm the previous books (the Bible).

- Muslims are instructed to read and believe what is revealed in the Bible.

Yes, it is true that there are also verses in the Qur'an that directly contradict the truth about Jesus and the Bible. But this only proves beyond any doubt that the writing of the Qur'an was not inspired by God. God would not contradict truths that He has already revealed in the Bible.

Jesus had just revealed to me how to share the gospel openly with Muslims: First, start with the verses in the Qur'an that speak favorably about Jesus and the Bible, then use those verses as a bridge to show Muslims that their own book is telling them to read and believe the Bible and to follow its teachings. It also clearly commands them to believe in, and to follow and obey Jesus. I was confident that Muslims could be convinced to read the Bible. I would then be able to teach Muslims the truth about Jesus using the Bible without inciting objections or anger. I was eager to get back to Afghanistan to try out this method.

Back to Afghanistan in 2008

When I returned to Afghanistan in 2008, I again stayed at the same guesthouse as the previous trip. This time I came with a much better knowledge of Islam, Muhammad, and the Qur'an, as well as an improved grasp of the language. In addition, and most importantly, I was armed with the rudimentary beginnings of a new method for sharing the gospel with Afghans that wouldn't immediately lead to arrest, persecution, or death. Equipped with a Qur'an in the local language (Dari), and some New Testaments in Dari, I spent a lot of my time on the streets and in the markets talking to anyone who was willing to converse with me. Although my language skills were unpolished, I was able to start a conversation discussing what the Qur'an said about Jesus and the Bible. Then I would invite the Muslims I spoke with to receive a New Testament to read and discuss.

Most days there were further language lessons with Amir, and I would ask him specific questions about words I needed to use for my daily sharing of the gospel in the city. Amir was very confused when I told him I was sharing the gospel message about Jesus with Muslims I met in taxis and in markets. Amir said that he had always been told by the missionaries that he should not try to share the gospel with Muslims or even with his own family. When I asked him how his family could be saved if he didn't tell them about Jesus, he was even more confused. Nobody had ever suggested his family could be saved too. I encouraged Amir to start to speak with his family and friends about Jesus, and then showed him how to start such a conversation using verses in the Qur'an that mentioned Jesus. He was very shocked and intrigued when I pointed him to the Qur'an verses that spoke favorably about Jesus and the Bible. He was excited to hear that there was a way to share Jesus with Muslims without the risk of being cut off from his family, or worse, violence.

I shared the gospel with many Muslims, and I was repeatedly surprised to find that I could be quite bold about Jesus without receiving any negative feedback. I could tell that many were shocked to hear someone speaking openly about Jesus, an experience that simply didn't happen publicly in Afghanistan. In fact, many Afghans were quite curious and eager to engage in a discussion, and they were just as eager to receive a New Testament in Dari when I offered it. I had been told by several of the Christian leaders that Afghans could be arrested and put in prison for even having a Bible in their possession. I think someone forgot to tell the Afghans that. When they received a New Testament from me most of them made no attempt to conceal it or act guilty about having it. I knew that using this contextualized approach was making sharing the gospel much more effective.

Through a couple from Oklahoma and an Afghan living in Canada I was able to connect with two Afghan families, all of whom were believers. I often met with these families to worship and study the Bible. One of the families lived near where I was staying, and we had a weekly Bible study together. While I led the study initially, after the second meeting I asked the parents to take the lead so they would get experience teaching from the Bible. They took turns leading the study each week and Jesus highly honored their efforts so much that within only a couple of weeks they were doing a wonderful job teaching from the Bible.

It is truly amazing how being saved and becoming followers of Jesus changes the dynamics in an Afghan family. Typically, if a man visits an Afghan in their home, especially if he is a foreigner, he will never see the man's wife or female children. He would typically be restricted to staying in one room with the man and his sons. The women would cook, and he would hear them in other parts of the house but would never see them. With families of born-again Christian Afghans, the dynamic was quite different with the entire family present when I visited. We all fellowshipped together and ate together. There was no gender separation or foreigner separation imposed. The freedom they clearly felt was palpable.

Christian vs. *Follower of Jesus* — Not Just Semantics

It wasn't long before I learned not to refer to myself as a Christian while in Afghanistan. I also recommended to the Afghan believers that they should not call themselves Christians. Instead, I referred to Christians as "Followers of Jesus" because when a Muslim hears the term Christian, an immediate bias is formed. What readily comes to their minds are culturally charged negative terms, such as infidel or kafir (a derogatory word for an infidel often used to refer to Christians). These terms encompass the firm beliefs that all Christians are war mongers, believe in three gods, are prone to excessive drinking, watch pornography, support abortion, don't pray or fast, and are not committed to the true faith of Jesus. Although not true, those things are what Muslims have been taught all their lives about Christians. When a foreign missionary tells a Muslim that they are a Christian, they are in essence communicating to the Muslim that they are ungodly and sinful, resulting in the Muslim immediately disrespecting and abhorring them. They generally will not immediately show those feelings, instead they will be very polite, but they won't believe or take seriously anything that the Christian says or believes.

It is very rare that an Afghan Christian would tell a Muslim that he converted to Christianity, since it is the same as saying that he is a traitor to his country, his people, and to Islam. He will be immediately seen as an infidel and could be subject to severe persecution, imprisonment, or murder. That is the main reason many foreign missionaries and Afghan believers felt it too dangerous to speak to Muslims about Jesus.

Whenever I met Afghans referring to themselves as Christian, I would always ask them to share their testimony. Almost without exception they would begin with the words, "I converted to Christianity in ____" (whatever year they *became* a Christian).

Since the protocol for foreign missionaries was not to share the gospel with anyone who they have not known well for three to seven years, and even then, to only answer specific questions, very few Afghans could have acquired enough gospel understanding to have been truly saved. For various reasons, such as securing a job working for the foreigners, or help leaving the country, some Afghans made the conscious decision to merely *change their religion*.

The decision to become a Christian for many Afghans simply meant abandoning Islam in practice and calling themselves a Christian. What was missing in this process was an understanding of Jesus, His divinity and sinlessness, and His death and resurrection. They did not understand the need for repentance and turning away from their sins, or how important it was to ask Jesus for forgiveness when they did sin. Very few Afghan Christians could even articulate the basic gospel message. So, when I met with them, I shared the gospel fully so that each person was clear on what it meant to be saved. Most of them accepted my invitation to repent and ask Jesus to forgive their sins and save them, and they made the decision to follow Jesus as Lord and trust in Him alone for their salvation. The need for me to do that with almost every Afghan Christian I met showed that many of the foreign missionaries had failed them. Obviously, a different approach and more thorough training in the gospel was crucial for establishing the body of Christ in Afghanistan.

I felt that the fear the missionaries shared about witnessing to Afghans, and the fear of even saying the name of Jesus, was something that could be replaced with new training using not only boldness, but a more comfortable and effective way of approaching the gospel. This was proven correct when I started to train the missionaries who were willing. Many of them were eager to learn how to share the gospel with Muslims.

During this trip to Afghanistan the Lord provided many wonderful opportunities to share the message of salvation with

Muslims and to train some of them to share the gospel with other Muslims. I was continually amazed at their openness and how well this new method for sharing the gospel was working. Many New Testaments and MP3 players with the New Testament recorded in Dari were distributed during this mission trip.

Meeting with a Sunni Imam

After four months in Kabul, I returned home and immediately began preparations for another trip to Afghanistan. Jesus made it clear that I would be going back, although I didn't know exactly when. My goal was to assemble a training manual containing everything a follower of Jesus would need to effectively share the gospel with Muslims. Since the beginning of such a manual had been started, and could benefit with some practice using the material, I located a mosque nearby in Dallas. I reasoned that it would be good experience to visit a Muslim leader to gauge how well the training material might be received.

The mosque turned out to be a Sunni Mosque, which means the leader is an "Imam" (with Shia Muslims, the title would be "Mullah"). Generally Sunni Muslims are more devoted to Islam and will be more opposed to Christianity than Shia Muslims. I spoke with the Imam and told him that I had been reading the Qur'an and had some questions.

We spent about two hours together. I discovered the Imam believed that Jesus did not die, that Jesus was not the Son of God, and that the Bible had been changed and corrupted. I then walked him through the verses in the Qur'an that I had discovered, verses that speak positively about Jesus and the Bible. Two hours later, without even going into the Bible yet, he had changed his beliefs substantially. He was now willing to agree that according to the Qur'an, Jesus did die and was raised to life again, and the Bible had to be true and correct. He even said that he could now understand why Christians called Jesus the Son of God.

An interesting thing happened when I pointed out certain verses in the Qur'an to the Imam. After reading one of the verses, the Imam paused and looked up at me. He looked like someone who had seen a ghost. I asked him why he looked so surprised. He looked at me and I could tell that he was struggling with whether he should tell me what he was thinking. Finally, he blurted out in frustration, "I've spent 14 years of my life studying in various mosques and Islamic religious schools throughout the world. I speak five languages fluently, and I have memorized, word for word, the entire Qur'an from beginning to end. But I have never seen this verse before in the Qur'an. I have it memorized word for word, but I swear that I have never noticed or understood the meaning of this verse before."

I then pointed out to him other verses in the Qur'an that also conflicted with what he had been taught about Jesus, the Bible, and Christian beliefs. He read those verses with the same surprise, saying again that he had no idea how he could have memorized these verses without having understood their meaning. So I explained to him that the Bible teaches us there is a spirit called antichrist which is opposed to Jesus—a spirit who can blind people from understanding the truth about Jesus until their eyes are opened by a more powerful spirit, the Holy Spirit of God. I then discussed how the Holy Spirit was opening his eyes to the truth, and if he was willing to receive the truth, then he should read the Bible to discover further truth about Jesus. My comments were obviously deeply affecting the Imam, who seemed to be uncomfortably convicted by them, so he rather abruptly ended our meeting.

I returned a couple of weeks later to deliver a Bible to him and I found him in his office. He did not take much time to speak with me, but I noticed a Bible on his desk. He had bought a Bible after our discussion and was reading it. During our brief conversation I sensed the Imam was struggling with what he was discovering. A highly learned and respected leader of a large mosque could not easily accept Jesus and tell others about Him being the Savior. That admission would almost certainly mean an end to all he had achieved as an Imam. Teaching the truth about Jesus would end his career and his exalted position would be lost. This is what Jesus spoke about as counting the costs. Many Muslims would like to embrace Jesus but find the cost too demanding.

Most of that winter was spent continuing my research on Islam and preparing the outline for the training manual. There were fourteen verses in the Qur'an that powerfully recognized Jesus and the Bible. These would be the foundation for the bridge method used to train believers to share the gospel with their Muslim families, friends, neighbors, and eventually even with strangers, and to encourage them to read and believe the Bible.

And Speaking of Counting the Cost

In preparation for my return to Afghanistan in 2009 I struggled to find a place to live. I had made reservations to stay at the guesthouse where I had stayed twice before. Unfortunately, the director of the organization had returned from the USA and heard I was openly sharing the gospel. A couple weeks before I was to leave, I received an email canceling my reservation and informing me that I was no longer welcome there. The email stated that the reason for the cancellation was because I was sharing the gospel with Muslims. Many of the Christian leaders in the area learned of my openness to share Jesus through this man. Unfortunately, these leaders did not understand the method I was using. They no doubt assumed I was using the typical and dangerous practice of speaking against Islam and Muhammad. I was now blacklisted and shunned.

It was early April, which is usually snow free in Kabul. But this year it was snowing the day I arrived, with several inches of fresh snow on the ground. I had arranged to rent a room at a place I found on the internet. It sounded good, but I quickly discovered it wasn't suitable. Kabul had been quite a bit warmer during March, so the oil heaters had been removed from all the rooms and I was freezing.

I called everyone I knew in the city. Finally, someone told me about another guesthouse run by a different Christian organization. The person running the guesthouse welcomed me and was willing to rent me a room for as long as I wanted. After a few days, he heard from one of the Christian leaders that I was in Afghanistan to share the gospel with Muslims and to train Afghans and missionaries to do the same. He asked to meet with me and asked me not to do any of that kind of work while I was staying at the guesthouse. I told him that if he was serious, I would have to find another place to stay, since Jesus had sent me to preach the gospel and train others. I promised him that I would hold off sharing the gospel and training until I found another place to stay. I was determined to keep my promise, but the next day he sent an employee to tell me I would have to leave the guesthouse immediately.

While aimlessly walking the streets I prayed to Jesus for assistance. On the street I ran into a Christian brother from the USA who I had met briefly at one of the foreigner meetings the previous year. We had lunch together and I told him I was looking for a place to stay for about seven months. I told him I needed to find a place fast, since I had to be out of the guesthouse right away. He told me he was renting a two-bedroom upstairs flat in a house owned by a Muslim couple who lived on the bottom floor. He offered to share his accommodation. I wanted to make sure my friend understood what I was doing in Afghanistan. I couldn't keep moving every few days when people found out I was evangelizing. I asked him if he would have a problem with my mission and he told me that he had no problem with what I was doing, and he even encouraged me. He told me I was free to do training at the house and to invite Afghans to the house to share the gospel with them. I moved in the next day and was very encouraged and delighted that Jesus had so quickly provided such a suitable place for me.

At that point I had the bulk of my research completed and I had most of the materials prepared. I still needed to finish the training manual to hand out or to email to anyone willing to receive it. Every day hours were spent writing, revising, and organizing all the material that had been collected. When writing and editing became tiring, I headed out to the streets to practice with the material, approaching taxi drivers and people in the markets. When I returned, I would tweak the material in the manual based on what I had experienced that day.

It took me a couple of months to finally complete the training manual. I had an Afghan friend take the manual to a printer to make copies. I gave free copies of the manual to all the missionaries and Afghan believers I knew who could speak and read English and I emailed copies to others. Then I emailed a copy to an Afghan believer I had met in 2008 and he agreed to translate the manual into Dari. Once he had finished the translation work the Dari version was printed and distributed to Dari-speaking Afghan believers.

In addition to preparing the training manual I also researched "Bible Storying." This is a method of sharing truth from the Bible by means of telling stories that are based on, and which carefully follow, stories found in the Bible. Some great Bible stories are suitable and appropriate for reaching Muslim seekers. The stories were compiled into a manual to accompany the training manual and it was also translated into Dari. I then created some short documents to be given to Muslims being witnessed to. All the materials combined formed what I felt was a comprehensive and effective set of materials to effectively evangelize the Muslim people.

The bridge method was designed to enable anyone to share the gospel of Jesus Christ with any Muslim they meet, friend or stranger, without *offending* the Muslim. This is not to say that some Muslims will not be offended by the gospel; in truth some will. The Bible itself says that some people will be offended by the gospel. The gospel is very simple and direct. At the heart of the Christian message is the clear teaching that the only way any man or woman can be saved and get to heaven is through repentance and faith in Jesus Christ as Savior and Lord. That is the core of Christian beliefs, and it is diametrically opposed to the common teachings of Islam about Jesus and salvation.

Some Christians feel that using the Qur'an in any way to help in sharing about Jesus with Muslims should not be done. They feel that it constitutes agreement with the Qur'an, giving the Qur'an credibility and authenticity. Whenever I have been criticized and accused of this, I always explain that the Qur'an is being used only as a tool, more specifically as a bridge. My goal is for the Muslim to understand that what they have previously heard about Jesus and the Bible is simply false because their own Qur'an confirms the Bible to be true and correct and, therefore, Jesus is the only way to heaven.

Exposing someone to an initial bridging experience usually takes anywhere from 15 to 30 minutes. After that, further time and discussion will take place using the Bible directly. Once we are focusing on the Bible, the Qur'an will only come back into the discussion if the Muslim asks questions about the Qur'an. Or I might refer to a verse from the Qur'an that speaks favorably about Jesus and the Bible when it is appropriate to interject it to support the Bible scripture being shared in the moment.

Occasionally I will encounter a Muslim well versed in the Qur'an, but this is quite rare. They might know and bring up certain other verses that contradict those Qur'an verses I am sharing with them. If that happens, arguing those points with the Muslim would be futile, as this same dialogue has been going on between Muslims and Christians for over 1400 years. Instead, the best reply is, "I have not studied those verses, so I cannot discuss them properly with you." And this will always be the truth, because the bridge method chooses to ignore those Qur'an verses that contradict the 14 verses favorably portraying Jesus and the Bible. However, I will advise them to ask a Mullah or Imam to explain why some verses in the Qur'an so clearly contradict each other. The Bible does not have such contradictions, which is one reason we know the Bible is true. That truth is so powerful for them to understand, because it means I am not there to argue with them or to insult Islam and disrespect Muhammad or the Qur'an. I am there simply to share the truth about Jesus and salvation so they can be saved.

Spiritual Attacks

As I was putting the finishing touches on the training manual and preparing to have it printed and distributed, I came under an unusual spiritual attack. Suddenly there were several close calls from bicycles and kids almost colliding into me. I had so many close calls in a brief period that it became clear that satan and his demons were trying to stop me before I could get the training manual distributed. Given the unforgiving nature of AS, an impact from a bicycle or a bad fall could have been paralyzing. Once distribution of the training manual was finished the close calls from bicycles and running kids immediately stopped.

Chapter 20

Sharing the Gospel with Muslims

I was incredibly busy in Afghanistan during this mission trip. Not only was I working daily on the training manual, but I also taught English and about Jesus at both a children's school and to a group of young Afghan men in a construction office. In addition I held training seminars for Afghan believers and seekers in how to share the gospel. Traveling exclusively by public transportation (in order to have more interaction with the locals and opportunities to visit a variety of shopkeepers), this also kept me busy, as I was witnessing about Jesus even during my normal daily activities.

Taxi Drivers

Public transportation was one of the best ways for me to approach Muslims. On public transportation I was always meeting a new Muslim driver and new people to speak with. On a typical day I would walk out to the main road from the house and flag down a taxi and ask the driver to take me to the other side of the city. While on route, I used the time to tell the taxi driver about Jesus. When available I would use a shared taxi (a taxi driver will pick up anywhere from two to five men going in the same direction). The shared taxis were preferable because the other passengers could overhear my conversation with the driver about Jesus.

The many conversations with taxi drivers usually followed a similar pattern. They began with some pleasant conversation, asking if he had children, where he lived and the like. My Dari was not completely fluent, so the driver would ask why my speech was not perfect, and if I spoke Pashtu, the other language spoken in Afghanistan. My reply, of course, was that English was my primary language. At which point he would ask why, and I would tell him I was from the USA. This is how the rest of a typical conversation would go:

Driver: "Okay, but you're an Afghan, so your parents are from Afghanistan?"

Me: "No, my parents are from Canada."

Driver: "But, but... you are an Afghan, right?"

Me: "No, I am originally from Canada and then I moved to the USA. I'm not an Afghan at all."

Driver: "How can that be? You look 100% like an Afghan."

This conversation was repeated often, and the confusion of all the taxi drivers was compounded because I made it a point to wear traditional Afghan clothing, I am short in stature, as are many Afghans, and my skin darkens easily in the sun. My cultural transformation included a long beard and an Afghan style haircut. In a county where many of the men no longer have long beards, and often wear western clothes instead of traditional clothes (western clothes being cheaper), I looked more like an Afghan than many Afghans! My lack of fluency was the only indication I was a foreigner.

Once the taxi driver got over the initial shock of learning I was an American and not an Afghan, he would naturally ask me why I was in Afghanistan. My reply was that I was a teacher, which led to the next question: What did I teach? My response was always the same, I teach from the four books. This response always intrigued them, so they inevitably asked what the four books were. Imagine their shock when they learned my teachings were about the Qur'an, the Old Testament, Psalms, and the New Testament—the four books mentioned in the Qur'an.

Since they heard the Qur'an mentioned, their next question would be, "So you are a Muslim?" "I didn't say that," I would reply, "but if you are asking me if I am submitted to God, yes, I am fully submitted to God, and I follow the way of Jesus." When they heard the word Jesus they would state, "Oh, you're a Christian." My reply was always, "I didn't say that, because I am not what you think a Christian is. You think a Christian is an infidel, right?" "Oh yes," would always be the reply. Then I would say, "But I just told you that I am submitted to God. If I am submitted to God, how can I be an infidel?" At that point the taxi driver would get a very perplexed look on his face. He would shake his head in bewilderment knowing that it is not possible to be submitted to God and be an infidel.

At that stage of the conversation, I would help them out of their confusion by explaining, "I am not what you think a Christian is. I am clearly not an infidel, because I am submitted to God, *and* I am a follower of Jesus in obedience to God." Then I would ask,

"Do you read the Qur'an?" "Oh yes," they would always reply even though many of the taxi drivers are illiterate. What they mean is that they hear verses from the Qur'an read aloud when they go to the mosque or over the loudspeakers mounted on the mosques.

Then I would ask, "Do you know that the Qur'an says that all Muslims must follow and obey Jesus?" "WHAT!?," would be their shocked reply. "Oh yes," I would explain, "the Qur'an clearly teaches that Jesus is the straight path, and all Muslims must follow and obey Jesus. It also teaches that all Muslims must read and obey the previous books that came before the Qur'an. The previous books are the Old Testament, Psalms, and the New Testament, all books from the Bible. Having read the complete Qur'an three times, I can confidently tell you this is what it says about Jesus and the previous books. Have you ever read the previous books?"

"Oh no," would be the reply, "you can't get the previous books in Afghanistan." I would quickly say, "I have one with me right here." Then I would pull out a Dari New Testament from my pocket and ask, "Can you read?" Some would say they could read but many could not. I also had small MP3 players that only played the New Testament in Dari. I would offer them the New Testament or the MP3 player, but most often both. They always accepted them. When I gave them an MP3 player, I would ask them to pull over to the side of the road and put in the earbuds and then show them how to turn it on and off. And before leaving them I would make sure the MP3 was turned on and playing the New Testament. They drove off listening to the New Testament in their own language for the first time in their lives.

Terrorist Taxi Driver

One day I jumped into a taxi with a rough looking driver who was wearing a black turban—often a sign of either a Taliban member or a Taliban sympathizer. As per my usual routine, I engaged in conversation with the man by asking him how he was doing, did he have kids, how old were they, etc.

When he realized I was an American I could see his facial expression immediately change to hatred. He became very quiet, and I could see that he was deep in thought. I am not naïve. I knew that he was probably thinking about the money he could get for me if he took me to one of the local Taliban leaders. Or maybe he was thinking of taking me somewhere where he and his friends would beat me and rob me or kill me. With murder in his eyes, he looked at me through the rear-view mirror and pointedly asked, "What are you doing in Afghanistan?"

After giving my response, which followed the typical conversation which led to the topic of Jesus, and as I told him more about Jesus and prepared the MP3 for him to listen to, the hatred and murder completely left his eyes. His angry face turned into a big smile. When we arrived at my destination, we exchanged telephone numbers (at his request) and he did not want to take money from me. I had to insist several times that he accept my taxi fare. He drove off with the MP3 player turned on and cued to John 1:1. He had the earbuds in his ears hearing for the first time in his life the Word of God in his own language. I knew how close I had come to being thrown into the hands of the Taliban, but it was worth it because he now had the opportunity to be saved.

The Shopkeepers

Many trips into the markets in Kabul were made, going from shop to shop to try and start conversations. Most people would speak to me only briefly, as many had a very low interest in spiritual things. Being persistent, I approached many people seeking those with the time and interest to engage in a spiritual conversation.

One day I met a young shopkeeper in a bookstore with whom I was able to immediately start a conversation about Jesus. When I told him that the Qur'an said Muslims must follow and obey

Jesus, he immediately ran out into the street and shouted out to someone to come quickly. I thought he might be calling for the authorities to arrest me. Instead, he was calling out to a friend of his in another shop to come and hear what I was saying. Both young men listened intently as I once again delved into the positive things that the Qur'an said about Jesus and the Bible. After sharing the gospel with them I offered them both a copy of the New Testament, which they readily accepted. When I returned to the bookseller's shop a few days later it was very surprising to see the Dari New Testament on the counter right in the front of the store, in plain view of any passerby. The reported potential for arrest from possessing the Bible once again appears unfounded.

The bookseller and I became good friends. He often asked me for more New Testaments because he had other friends who also wanted to read it, so whenever I went to see him, I always brought extras. Even though I suspected he might be selling them to interested customers, I assumed there was probably no better person to be distributing the Word of God than a bookseller in Kabul.

Just down the street from the bookseller was another young man who owned a flower shop. He also was interested when I started to talk to him about Jesus and the Bible, and we had many conversations. Often one or more of his workers and friends from other shops nearby would drop in and join us in our conversations. They would also take me to other shops to meet their friends, and the flower seller and the bookseller were regular stops for me.

One day when I visited the flower shop both the flower seller and his partner were there. With them was a young man who occasionally helped them and who I had met a couple times before. Previously the young helper had not been interested in Jesus at all, but this time he joined in our discussion and showed a lot of interest by asking questions. I knew that Jesus was working on their hearts, and they were discussing Jesus among themselves when I was not there. They asked many questions about Jesus, and the young helper asked me why Christians say that Jesus is the Son of God when the Qur'an says that God has no son. It took me only a few minutes to answer this often-asked question because it had been studied extensively for the training manual. They listened intently, nodding, and voicing their understanding.

Understanding these things about Jesus was all very new to them. Previously they would just reject Christian beliefs outright because of stumbling blocks such as Jesus being referred to as the Son of God. Once they got over the stumbling blocks, often their ears and hearts were very open to hearing the message of salvation. But taking that final step to becoming a follower of Jesus is very difficult for a Muslim to do. It is not something they take lightly or readily, and they will often consider it for a long time before taking the steps to being born again in Christ.

Another Muslim man whom I visited regularly owned a convenience store along with his father. The father never wanted to talk much, but his son was the opposite and we conversed a long time during our first meeting. Every time I visited him we would talk about Jesus and the Bible, and I gave him a New Testament and an MP3 player. After several meetings he said he wanted to read the entire Bible, so on my next visit I brought him a copy of the entire Bible in Dari. He had many questions and I had much to tell him, so when I visited, we would talk for hours while people entered and left his shop.

It was a very busy convenience store. He knew most of the customers well as most of them worked or lived close by. Whenever a customer came in, we would pause our conversation and he would tell the customer that I was a follower of Jesus. Often, he would engage them in a conversation about Jesus, sharing many of the things he learned from our discussions. Whenever that occurred, I was always amazed. I had not seen such boldness even among the Afghan believers. Here was a Muslim who had not yet accepted and received Jesus having open conversations with many of his customers about Jesus and the Bible. He even showed his customers the Dari Bible. This was even more confirmation that Afghans are eager to discuss Jesus and the Bible if they are initially approached in a respectful manner.

During one visit he told me that Muslims believe there have been 124,000 prophets since Adam. I didn't argue with him. Instead, I asked him, "Of all the 124,000 prophets you believe in, how many of them are alive today? Only one, Jesus! How many of the 124,000 prophets you believe in were born of a virgin? And how many gave sight to blind people and healed people with leprosy? How many raised the dead? One, Jesus! How many died, were put in a tomb, and three days later rose from the dead and are alive today? Only Jesus!" Logic dictated that he had to agree with me that of all the prophets, whatever their number, only one stands out above all the rest and only one is still alive—Jesus! It was clear that he was now at the threshold of accepting and receiving Jesus as Savior and Lord.

The Fourth Brother

Another memorable event happened when I was in another convenience store that I frequently visited near to where I was living. There were three brothers running the store, always sitting behind the counter. They were tribal Sunni Muslims, the Afghan group most opposed to Christianity. I never had any success in engaging the three brothers in conversation, but this time I met a young man who was the fourth brother. He was much younger than the other three and much more willing to speak with me.

At a small counter next to where the three brothers were sitting, the younger brother and I had an hour-long conversation where I explained what the Qur'an said about Jesus and the Bible, and what the Bible taught about the gospel and how to be saved. I pointed out that the Qur'an stated all Muslims should be reading the Bible and following Jesus. I told him that my purpose in coming to Afghanistan was to call Muslims back to the true faith. Not the faith of their traditions, but the faith revealed in the Bible.

I further explained that by not reading the Bible and following Jesus, they were missing the most important part of what they are supposed to be believing and following. He thanked me for coming to Afghanistan and he told me that I was doing a good thing for Muslims by calling them back to the true faith.

When sharing the gospel, I am focused and passionate and tend to be oblivious to my surroundings. But suddenly in the middle of preaching the gospel to this young man in the aisle I looked around. On one side of me I saw a group of shoppers, about five or six people listening to every word and most apparently deeply engrossed in what I was saying. I then looked to the other side of me and realized the three older brothers were staring at me and listening intently as well.

My thought at that moment was, "Uh oh Lord, did I push it too far?" Then I heard the voice of the Holy Spirit say to me, "No, you keep preaching the gospel. I have your back." So, I continued sharing the gospel, making sure I was very clear, concise, and sufficiently loud, since I now realized there was a larger audience. When I finished speaking to the young man, I gave him a New Testament and an MP3 player, and he was listening to it when I left. I went back to the store a couple of days later and asked the young man if he was still listening to the New Testament. "Oh yes!" He replied. "It is wonderful to hear and understand about the Bible."

Rickshaws

Another terrific way to evangelize without difficulty was when riding in a motorized rickshaw. The rickshaws are a very inexpensive way to travel for shorter distances. They consist of a metal box built around a motorcycle.

The driver sits on the motorcycle seat and directly behind him is a bench seat where three people can sit side by side. This is where the women sit. Behind that row of seats are two bench seats perpendicular to the front row seats and facing each other. Up to three men can sit on each of these bench seats, so the maximum capacity including the driver is a total of ten people. The rickshaws are open to anyone to ride. Often the driver will wait at an intersection until the rickshaw is full of people before leaving. On route he will drop people off and pick up other people.

One day I was in the back of a rickshaw with three Afghan men. There were three women sitting in the bench seat in front of us. I announced to them I was a follower of Jesus, and quickly added, "The Qur'an says that Jesus knows the way to heaven and that Muslims should follow the way of Jesus." At this remark the women in the front turned in unison and looked back at me with startled and curious looks on their faces. The women *never* look at the men. Instead, as is their custom, they ignore them. This response was extremely unusual to see and what they did would be considered a grave cultural faux pas. But the women clearly just had to see who this man was who was speaking about Jesus in such a way.

The three men started talking among themselves. They were saying things like, "What is this new teaching? What does he mean he is not what we think a Christian is but is a follower of Jesus? Why is he speaking about the Qur'an?" There was no anger or outrage. Their response was a curious questioning about what this might mean to them. How awesome it was to bear witness to this!

On several occasions, when there were no other people in the rickshaw, I would sit in the row behind the driver and share the gospel with him. Every time when leaving the rickshaw, I would make sure that the driver would have an MP3 player turned on with the earbuds in his ears listening to the New Testament in Dari. Sometimes while walking on the sidewalk, I would spot a rickshaw going past me with my MP3 earbuds in the driver's ears. As he drove by, I would pray that the Word of God would touch him and that he and his family would be saved.

Encounters like this continued to encourage me to train Afghan believers how to share about Jesus using the bridge method.

Muslims are opposed to Christianity, but they are not opposed to Jesus. It is good news to them when they hear that they can follow and obey Jesus, who the Qur'an says knows the way to heaven, without having to *become a Christian* or without having to bear all the negative things the word Christian implies to them in their culture. Personally, I don't care how the saved refer to themselves. If they repent and accept and receive Jesus as Savior and Lord and read the Bible and follow its teachings, does it really matter what they call themselves? If calling yourself a Christian in Afghanistan and other Muslim countries triggers others to consider you to be an immoral traitor, then they aren't going to open their hearts to Jesus. Instead, if you call yourself a Follower of Jesus, then Muslims will not automatically see you negatively. It was a new light for Afghanistan: Jesus was coming in power, love, and humility, not through a set of strict religious rules and protocols!

Surviving Ramadan on the Mission Field

Ramadan is a tense and stressful time for Muslims. During Ramadan, which lasts about one month, Muslims must fast during the daylight hours. They are not even supposed to drink water, and when it is especially hot and dusty, it becomes a time of great discomfort and suffering. Often tempers flare and people are easily angered.

One afternoon I was sitting in the back of a rickshaw waiting for the driver to depart. I overheard the driver get into an argument with the driver of another rickshaw and the two arguing drivers started yelling curses at each other. Suddenly our driver stormed off from the argument in a rage. He jumped in the rickshaw and immediately sped off, hitting a very deep pothole at a high rate of speed. There are no effective shock absorbers on the rickshaws, so even on a smooth road the ride is bumpy. Hitting that deep pothole at high speed was mind-jarring and exceptionally painful.

I have severe osteoporosis from the prednisone that treats my Crohn's disease, and my bones are very brittle as a result. Immediately the pain in my neck and spine became more intense than usual. But since I had lived with intense pain continuously for much of my life, I ignored it and carried on. It wasn't until a couple months later after returning to the USA when the pain in my neck hadn't lessened that I went to a doctor for x-rays and an MRI. The results showed that I had compression fractures in three vertebrae in my neck and two in my back. The MRI also showed that I had a piece of a vertebra in my neck impinging into my spinal column, which was the source of the more intense pain. I tried to avoid being in Afghanistan during Ramadan after that experience. Muslims are too stressed from the fasting to be open to any new interactions.

My trips to Afghanistan were difficult times for me physically. In addition to constant and extreme pain from AS (ankylosing spondylitis), while in Kabul my Crohn's disease would flare up acutely. Crohn's is a terrible disease. When inflammation is at a high point it is very painful, and you have a horrible feeling of deep sickness in your gut and always need to be near a toilet. I was continually fatigued and desperately ill. Because of Kabul's bad air quality, I also had to deal with at least one bout of uveitis in my eyes during each trip. This barrage of maladies reminded me that it was only the grace of God and the desire to obey Jesus that enabled me to continue serving Him in Afghanistan.

Chapter 21

Training Others to Share the Gospel

Once I finished preparing the training manual I began meeting many Afghans who were interested in hearing about Jesus and the Bible. In fact, so many were interested it was overwhelming, but in a good way since it meant that many Afghans were being drawn to Jesus. Afghan believers, hungry to hear more about the Word of God, were coming for training. While this assured me Jesus was drawing Afghans to Himself, there was a grave shortage of workers. Workers willing to take risks to help people receive salvation and enter the Kingdom of God were needed, and they needed the training to effectively reach the entire Afghan population. As Jesus said when He walked the earth: "*The harvest truly is plentiful, but the laborers are few.*" [Matthew 9:37].

Combating the Fear Disease

When training believers to share the gospel, one of my greatest challenges was addressing and combatting fear. I would advise them not to give into fearful thoughts to avoid catching the "fear disease." Once that disease is caught, it is very difficult to cure yourself. Left unchallenged, fear intensifies until it eventually kills most of your faith.

Fear is the enemy of faith, and the brother of fear is death. These truths were painfully obvious in Afghanistan. The Christian leaders and the missionaries in Afghanistan were very courageous warriors. They were willing to go into extremely dangerous places to show the love of Christ to the people, yet they were often filled with fear when it came to sharing the gospel. That fear of sharing the gospel was like a disease. It was irrational and unbecoming of a servant of Jesus. Being diligently *fearless* is a key to walking with Jesus.

Their fear was somewhat understandable since they did not yet have a way to share the gospel without immediately risking their safety and their lives. Still, I was very offended and angered by the influence satan had over many Christian leaders by making them fearful of even saying Jesus' name in public. One day I became so angry with satan that I took a taxi to the bottom of a very tall hill that overlooked the city. A large community of people lived there on the steep incline. I walked the many stairs and narrow streets that turned into donkey trails, until I got to the top of the hill. Then I shouted out multiple times as loud as I could both in Dari and in English, "Jesus is Lord!" It felt so good to shout His name over the city, letting satan and his hordes of demons know that regardless of the stranglehold of fear they had on the Afghan believers and many of the Christian workers, Jesus is Lord of Afghanistan. I declared that His name would no longer be portrayed as a fearful or shameful thing to say, but it will be proclaimed in faith throughout Afghanistan, and many will be saved.

Christians leaders are called to be examples to those they serve and teach. As such, they need to be like Daniel. Not just willing to be thrown into the lion's den, but willing to *voluntarily run* into the lion's den, knowing that the One who died for us is already there and waiting for us to demonstrate extraordinary faith. Jesus will be there standing at our side when we do. Thankfully, over the years the bridge method has become more widely used for sharing the gospel in Afghanistan.

Training a Group of Afghans

My friend whose apartment I was sharing introduced me to another believer in the construction business. Bill was from the USA and was working with a group of twelve young Afghan men, teaching them English, often using the Bible. Bill was also helping some of them obtain scholarships to study in the USA. Bill and I hit it off immediately. He was very bold in sharing about Jesus and the Bible with the young men he was training. At our first meeting I gave him a copy of my training manual. When I returned a few days later he told me that it was the best material he had ever read on how to share the gospel with Muslims. I asked him if he would be interested in allowing me to train his group of Afghans. He thought it a great idea and so they began their training in the bridge method.

My goal was to follow the pattern described by the Apostle Paul in his second letter to Timothy: *"And the things that you have heard from me among many witnesses, commit these to faithful men who will be able to teach others also."* [2 Timothy 2:2]. I knew these men needed to be trained to not only enable them to share the gospel with others, but also equip them to train others. This would be the only way to train more people than I could manage myself.

During the initial meeting with the class, I soon identified the man who was best comprehending my teaching. At the end of that first session, I asked him to teach the next class. He reacted with shock and disbelief. "But you are the teacher," he said. "I have not yet learned what you are teaching." "There is no better way to learn than to teach," I replied, "and you are wrong about me being the teacher. The real teacher is Jesus through the Holy Spirit. And the Holy Spirit is just as capable of teaching through you as He is through me." I showed him which part of the training manual to focus on to prepare himself for the next week's teaching.

I also told him to pray to Jesus asking for assistance and Holy Spirit anointing.

The following week, as this young man was teaching, it was all I could do to keep from weeping with joy throughout the entire session. The Lord had clearly anointed him. After the class we spoke, and he said he didn't know where some of his words came from. He said it was like someone else was speaking through him. I told him that it was the Holy Spirit speaking and teaching through him and I advised him to always ask the Holy Spirit to be the One in control of his teaching.

After that second meeting I told him he would again teach next week and that he should choose one of the other men and train him to teach as well. The goal was that by the time the training was complete each man there would have had the chance to be the teacher. Through this method each man there would be equipped not only to share the gospel with Muslims, but they would also be able to teach others how to do the same. It was such an answer to prayer to see Afghan believers being raised up to train other Afghan believers. That had been my goal right from the start, and seeing this vision in action was such a huge blessing. I was thrilled!

As word got around about the bridge method, some of the missionaries who supported what I was doing would give my phone number to Afghans they knew to be believers. They would call and I would arrange to meet with them and their groups for training. Or they would come and train with me one-on-one and then they would train their groups of believers.

I also started an English Discussion Class for some of the local men who wanted help learning English. Of course, all our lessons and class discussions were about Jesus and the Bible, and I had many wonderful conversations with the men who attended the classes.

Chapter 22

The Significance of the Pickle

Life-Changing Impacts Are Not Only for the Muslim

One of my favorite songs from my younger days was a folk song that spoke about the significance of a pickle. While the song writer created an actual pickle in the telling of his story, the "pickle" was also a euphemism for finding yourself in a problematic set of circumstances such as *being in a pickle*. And I was in a pickle before the Lord sent me the solution of the bridge method, which cleared a path around a rather significant roadblock. So too, the following people I met while in Afghanistan found themselves in a bit of a pickle, but subsequently their paths cleared, their lives forever altered.

Rashid

One of the young men in the training group was really on fire for Jesus. His name was Rashid, and he was very excited about the training. He was attending university and eager to share the gospel with Muslims he knew there. He asked me for some personal training, so we met a couple days a week. At our first meeting Rashid showed me an outline he had written about plans for the advancement of the Christian religion in Afghanistan. I smiled and told him that what I would be teaching him had nothing to do with religion, but everything to do with Jesus. His plans would soon change when he received more training as a Follower of Jesus.

When Rashid came to the house, we would study the Bible and pray together. I gave him a solid foundation in the gospel, more practice and training on how to share the gospel, and a better understanding of what it means to be sold out for Jesus. Rashid was bold and passionate about Jesus, and it was a pleasure to teach him more each week. We went out some days together to share the gospel in taxis and on the streets. We would also use the group taxis so we could share with the driver and the other passengers at the same time. I encouraged Rashid to be baptized, which he did along with several of the other men in Bill's group. The baptism was a wonderful time of celebration and fellowship.

Young Afghan Believer Shares with His Family

The bridge method proved itself repeatedly to be an effective tool for both the missionaries and the Afghan believers. One example was the young Afghan man I hired to translate my training manual. He had become a believer about two years previously while in India. After becoming a Christian, he went back to his family in Afghanistan to tell them the Good News. He told his family that he had changed his religion, he was rejecting Islam, rejecting Muhammad, and now he was a Christian. He assumed his family would listen to him and immediately abandon Islam and become Christians too. However, as usually happens, his family did not embrace what he was telling them about Jesus. Instead, they were extremely angry with him, and it created a huge rift between him and his family that led to threats from his father.

Consequently, they would not allow him to read the Bible at home, and to remain in their home he was required to go to the mosque with the family for prayer.

While translating the training manual he was exposed to the bridge method. He took what he had learned while translating and asked to speak with his father about it. He showed his father the Qur'an verses that spoke positively about Jesus and the Bible. His father agreed that the Qur'an does say that Muslims should read the Bible and that Muslims must follow and obey Jesus. Not only does he now have his father's blessings to read the Bible at home, but he has also had some deep discussions with his father about Jesus. The once-closed door is now wide open to discuss Jesus with his other family members.

A Random Pastor Overcomes Fear

One day I met with a pastor from the US who was living and working in Afghanistan. He contacted me when he learned from someone about the training and wanted me to train him and an Afghan brother who works with him. I had met them briefly when I was there in 2008. The pastor reminded me that when we previously met, I told the Afghan brother that in giving into his fear he was forgetting the power of God to answer prayer and change hearts. He told me that those simple words had impacted both of their lives in a very profound way over the past year and they both had overcome their fears and were eager to be trained in how to share the gospel with Muslims. It is amazing how just a few simple words can be used by the Lord in such mighty ways.

The Attorney General's Prosecutor

One day I got a telephone call from a man who identified himself as a prosecutor from the Attorney General's Office in Kabul. I was shocked when he told me who he was, but then he said he was a believer, and someone had told him about me. He asked me to disciple and train him. I immediately agreed though I considered the possibility that I was being set up. Was I about to be arrested? Then I was reminded of when Jesus told Ananias to go and meet with Saul, and Ananias said, and I am paraphrasing here, "But, but, but... you must be kidding Lord? He's one of the bad guys!" I am still amazed that the Lord brought a man from that office to be discipled. But with all the amazing things I have seen Jesus do, it didn't surprise me at all when unexpected events like this happened.

John's Prison Ministry

One of the people I trained was a missionary from the USA named John, who had served the Lord in Afghanistan for quite a few years and was fluent in Dari. He also spoke Pashtu as well. John came to me for training in the bridge method. He was very excited about the new possibilities that it opened for him to share the gospel more freely and overtly than he had been doing.

Shortly after the training John was arrested (not for sharing the gospel, but for something else), and he spent three months in a local jail. I can't even imagine the horrible conditions that he endured for those three months. Gratefully, Jesus had given him a short-term prison ministry while he was incarcerated. Below is a copy of the email I received from John after he was released from prison:

> *Garry, May God bless you! I was recently wrongly imprisoned in Kabul for three months and had numerous (probably nearly a hundred) testimonies of sharing my faith with local Muslims, mullahs, scholars, and workers. Using much of what I learned in your class. Laying hands on many, praying for healing. Worshiping and sharing with them what I was saying. Whenever I would talk about the Love of Christ in the conversation their hearts would begin to melt and even the hardest of them would have an open and intriguing response. Nothing can resist the Love of Christ when it is shared in truth, they just need to hear it! I am so excited about sharing to Muslim's wherever I am now. God bless you! —Your Brother, John*

It was so encouraging to receive positive reports like this from dear brothers and sisters who used the bridge method to share the gospel with Muslims. This news helped me to stay focused. Seeing the incredibly positive effect on their witness gave me much needed energy and desire to continue training as many as were willing.

Chapter 23

The Vision

After being in Afghanistan for seven months I headed back home at the end of October, where once again I spent most of my time preparing to return to Afghanistan whenever Jesus told me the time was right. While at home it occurred to me that once Afghan believers were trained and equipped to share the gospel with Muslims, it would be helpful if these believers had a reason to gain access into the homes of their neighbors, or even strangers. The vision the Lord provided to me was brilliant. However, I would later discover that Jesus had another purpose behind the vision that was wholly different than the one I had assumed. In retrospect I can see that guiding me the way He did was required for His plan to be successful. I have said it many times before, and I am sure I will say it many times again, Jesus is brilliant and all His plans are wonderful!

The vision included the manufacturing of bio-sand water filters and supplying them to Afghan families. The water in Kabul is terrible. People have city water or shallow wells, both of which are extremely unhealthy. Most people can't afford bottled water, so poor families must drink whatever water is available and it is often contaminated. The infant mortality rate in Afghanistan is extremely high. Much of it is fueled by diseases and other issues directly related to contaminated water. The vision was to set up a small manufacturing facility in Kabul where concrete bio-sand water filters would be manufactured and distributed. They would be sold at a very low price of USD$12, which was below the cost to make them, and we would provide financing at one dollar a month for a year. After installing the water filter, an Afghan believer would come back to pick up their monthly payment and service the filter. This plan would afford multiple opportunities to visit the family and develop friendships, with the goal to share about Jesus.

In 2011 I attended another conference for missionaries and organizations that served in Afghanistan. As before, I was again struggling to find residence in Kabul for my upcoming trip because my friend's family was now living with him and there was no room in the apartment for me. The Lord gave me a divine connection at this conference. It was there that I met Werner and Hannelie, who had been serving in Afghanistan for about eight years. They were excited to hear of my experiences of boldly sharing the gospel. We were most definitely of like mind, and we hit it off right away. They offered to help me find accommodations when I came to Afghanistan, and I was overjoyed. I was looking forward to seeing them again when Jesus told me to return to Kabul.

Chapter 24

Final Trip to Afghanistan

The call to return came, and I arrived back in Afghanistan in April of 2011. I called Werner from the airport. As one of the country leaders of a non-profit organization working in Afghanistan, Werner was also involved in various ministries. Hannelie served as a medical doctor. They had rented a house which they used as an office, and they had several Afghan office employees who were believers.

Werner showed me two small rooms above the garage. One room was furnished and occupied by one of Werner's Afghan workers. The other room was unfurnished and had a bare concrete floor. Between the two rooms was a small bathroom. Werner said, "I assume you don't want to stay here." "No, it's perfect," I replied. He looked at me and said, "Really? But it's not finished." "I will finish it." I said. "I'll put carpet on the floor and buy some furniture." "Okay," he said, "if you think you can make it work, you can stay here." "It's perfect," I repeated. And it was perfect. I was so thankful that Jesus had exceeded my expectations. I had a private room big enough for a bed and a desk and a few pillows to sit on when I had guests. In addition, I could use the kitchen in the office. I was blessed to share the bathroom with only one other person. I could not have been happier if it had been a 5-star hotel.

I moved in right away and the journey began. One of the first things I did was to sit down with Werner for a heart-to-heart conversation about my plans. I told him that my goal was to share the gospel with every Muslim who would listen to me, and I shared my plans for training others to share the gospel as well. I also told him of my intent to seek out Mullahs and other Muslim religious leaders, to see what their reaction would be to my sharing the gospel openly with them. I told Werner that I felt the Lord encouraging me to push the limits to determine how far I could go without experiencing serious efforts to stop me, and I naturally expected pushback that could possibly lead to some serious trouble.

I offered to start looking for another place to stay if he was uncomfortable with my plan. Werner told me that when he and his family made the decision to come to Afghanistan nine years previously, they knew the danger they faced. He said they had counted the cost, and they were all prepared to give up their lives if necessary to help see the gospel of salvation come to the Afghans. He said that he supported me sharing the gospel and training others to do the same. He encouraged me to be as bold as I wanted to be, and to feel free to bring people to the office to share the gospel with them and to train them.

I also told Werner about my plans for the water filter project, and that I was looking for a place where I could manufacture the filters. He thought it was a great idea and he offered to let me use part of the yard on the office property for my work area. I was extremely pleased with the setup.

A Promising Start - Then a Hiccup

I ordered two metal molds to make the concrete water filters. Within a few weeks the molds were delivered, and I hired a local Afghan brother to work with me. My new worker said he was not expecting to do manual labor and disliked getting his hands dirty, so he quit the first day. The next person I hired was one of the Afghan believers who had been training with me the previous year. He mistakenly thought he would only have to supervise others doing the work and he also didn't like to get his hands dirty, so he quit on his first day too.

Confused, I asked the guys in the office what they thought was causing the dilemma I was facing. They explained that in Afghanistan there is an unspoken caste system. It was not immediately obvious, but every Afghan knew and worked with a strong cultural bias regarding physical labor. I was informed that my first mistake was asking these men to do physical labor. In Afghanistan all physical work and chores around the household are done by women and girls. Since women are not allowed to associate with men other than their relatives, any physical work done outside the household is therefore done by men from the lowest class. An educated male would consider any physical labor to be demeaning.

Werner was able to assist me by putting me in contact with the person who oversaw communication with the foreign missionaries. He told me that I should prepare an email asking for people to contact any Afghan believers they knew and tell them there was a job available with me if they wanted to work. I did as he suggested and received several replies.

This time I made sure to tell the Afghans who called that they would personally have to do heavy and dirty concrete work and they would have to get their hands dirty all day every day. Most said they would call me back later, but then never did. Finally, I received a call from an Afghan believer named Bashir who was living with his wife and kids about an eight-hour drive from Kabul. He asked me about the job, and after providing all the details, including the physical labor part, he was still interested. He told me he was accustomed to physical work and had no problem doing it. I invited him to come for an interview and he replied that he would come to Kabul the following week. After Bashir contacted me there were no further calls from other Afghans about the job. But the project could be started with just one worker and myself, so I was very encouraged and eager to get underway.

When Bashir had not arrived in Kabul within a week, I emailed him. One of his kids had been sick, but he promised to show up the following week. A few days later while reading the Bible, the Lord sent me a shocking revelation—*He told me to halt the water filter project!* I could not make sense of this command since I knew Jesus had encouraged me all along. Now Jesus was telling me to shut it down? I was very confused. I chose to ignore the message and continued my devotions, only to hear the Lord speak again. This time there was no doubt in my mind that this was Jesus. He said to me very clearly: "Shut down the water filter project."

Did Jesus Really Change His Mind or Change Mine?

"What? Shut it down? You've got to be kidding Lord!" I had spent over a year preparing for this project, and now that I was finally ready to be up and running, I was being told not to continue this pursuit. All my prayer partners had been told of the enormous potential to reach the lost, and funds had been donated for this project. I couldn't let them down. I cried out to the Lord saying, "I know I've had some problems getting Afghan believers to work on the project, but I have a worker coming any day now who says he is willing and eager to get started. What will I tell my prayer partners? What will I tell Werner since he provided the space for me to do this? What will I do with the molds that I just spent several thousands of dollars to purchase? Please Lord, I can do this. I can make this project a success." In earnest I passionately prayed all my arguments to try to get Jesus to change His mind. I did not want to experience the humiliation of having to tell everyone who had been excited about the project that now I was shutting it down for no good reason. "Shut it down," was all I heard in reply to these prayers. And then silence.

I knew from experience that once Jesus told me to do something, He was not going to change His instructions. It did not matter if I was humiliated or inconvenienced or thought I was right. I knew I had to shut the project down, but I was confused and embarrassed, even hesitant to announce the decision to anyone.

I first went to Werner to discuss this development, hoping he would understand. At first, he thought that I was shutting it down because I was discouraged at the first two workers not working out. Then he went through a list of reasons why I shouldn't give up on it. His reasons included most of the points that I had brought to Jesus. "I know Werner," I said, "I completely agree with you. If you knew me better, you would know that I never give up on a project no matter how difficult it might be, especially since Jesus told me to do it to begin with. But Jesus said to shut it down, so what else can I do?" He tried to reason with me to give it another chance, but I knew that I had heard from Jesus. I knew obedience was my only choice.

I was so embarrassed and humbled. Figuratively, I had my tail between my legs and a mouth full of crow as I wrote an email to my prayer partners. I informed them that the water filter project was now canceled. I explained it as best I could. I asked them to please email me and let me know if they had donated funds specifically for the water filter project, and I would immediately return those funds to them. Surprisingly, nobody emailed to ask for their funds back. Several people emailed me to say that they supported my decision, which was encouraging. Fortunately, I was able to sell the concrete molds to an organization doing clean water projects in Afghanistan and I recovered almost all the money I had spent.

That same day I sent an email to Bashir (subsequently I learned he never received it) informing him that the water filter project had been canceled and not to come for the interview. A couple of days later I got a call from Bashir telling me he had arrived in Kabul that morning. I opened my mouth to tell him that there was no longer a job because the water filter project had been canceled, when I very clearly heard Jesus say to me, "No! Don't say that. Invite him to come and meet with you." I gave directions to Bashir, and I told him to call me when he was outside the gate. I asked Jesus what this was all about but got no reply.

Before I tell you the rest of what happened I need to interject something here. Jesus had made it quite clear what He wanted me to do in Afghanistan. First, I was to find out how to share the gospel openly with Muslims without being immediately persecuted, arrested, or killed. And then I was to train others, especially the Afghan believers, to share the gospel with Muslims. I knew that I was not being called to spend my life as a missionary in Afghanistan, and the Lord's initial instruction was simply to "go and see." Thus, the work was more about gathering information based on my experiences there, information that I could pass on to the Afghan believers and the missionaries so they could reach Afghans with the gospel. I needed to identify how far one could go with evangelizing, and then find the Afghan believers and missionaries who were serious about following and obeying Jesus and train them to spread the gospel over the longer term. Over the years I had often asked Jesus to bring me into contact with an Afghan man who would become like a "Paul the Apostle" of Afghanistan. Someone who would take the gospel to many different areas of Afghanistan and lead the training and discipling of Afghan believers.

Bashir arrived at the house, and when I opened the gate and saw his face, Jesus said to me, "This is the man who you have been praying for all these years, your "Paul the Apostle" of Afghanistan. The man who you will train to preach the gospel and who will train others to do the same."

Overjoyed, I couldn't contain my excitement! I greeted Bashir and invited him in. I began by telling him all that had transpired. I told him that since he needed a job, I was going to offer him the same salary that he would have received to work on the water filter project, but instead I would be training him daily on how to share the gospel with Muslims. He was amazed and excited and couldn't wait to get started.

Training Bashir - The One Who Brings Good News

I praised Jesus for sending Bashir to me, and for the absolute brilliance He used to accomplish His plan. All that work preparing for the water filter project; all the research and planning; manufacturing the molds; all the humbling perceived failure—only to be discarded? Why? To prepare a way for me to meet Bashir and focusing my energies and resources on training him, without the distractions the water filter project would have created. In other words, His plan, not my plan, was now in place. And, like a symphony, the plan was well-orchestrated, with Jesus the conductor speaking forth His Word to move spiritual mountains and affect circumstances. And while it had certainly not come together as I planned, *it was His divine plan for achieving His goals.* It was abundantly clear that the Creator of the universe had been orchestrating every detail all along.

This realization was overwhelming. I had a clean slate with Bashir. A clean slate on which Jesus would build His apostle. I knew that Jesus' clear instructions were to train Bashir by building first a solid foundation of faith, hope, and love. I knew what I had to do, so I got to it, and I started training Bashir all day, five to six days a week.

We spent our first few days together just talking. We talked about our past and what we saw for the future in serving Jesus. I shared my vision for the gospel going out in boldness throughout Afghanistan. Bashir had the same vision, and he was very excited about being trained.

After Bashir was equipped enough to share the gospel using the bridge method, I asked him to help me get some fixtures and tiles for the bathroom. Between the squat toilet and climbing the stairs, both of my knees were so stressed I was having a tough time walking. Hoping to spare my knees, I planned to remove the squat toilet and replace it with a traditional sit-down toilet.

Bashir and I spent several hours buying a toilet and tile and finding workers to do the job. Then we went to a restaurant for lunch and took a taxi on the way back. I had previously told Bashir about how I always talked to the taxi drivers about Jesus and the Bible. Guess what Bashir did in the taxi on the way back? Yes, he did! He had a great conversation with the taxi driver about Jesus and the Bible and without any coaxing from me. A few days later when the tile setter was finishing the job, I mentioned what the Qur'an said about the Bible. He was interested, so Bashir took it from there and started to talk to him about Jesus and the Bible. This was the first time I had seen an Afghan believer talk to a stranger about Jesus, and Bashir was doing it willingly.

But our work together was not without its problems; satan clearly saw us as a threat and tried to break us apart by snatching the vision right out of Bashir's heart using some of the Afghan office workers at Werner's office. They all professed to be Christians and one of them was the purported leader of the church in Afghanistan. Werner encouraged these men to be bold in sharing the gospel and to take my training, and Werner himself certainly did not follow the accepted protocols limiting evangelism. Yet in private the men argued with me persistently, trying to convince me to stop sharing the gospel with Muslims. And they also objected to me bringing other Afghans to the office for training. They were filled with fear, and it was a constant battle to keep focused on the work while being constantly criticized.

These men were also feeding Bashir negative comments about me whenever I was not in the room. It is too dangerous to share the gospel in Afghanistan, they claimed, until Bashir's heart also became filled with fear. For several days he did not show up for our training, nor did he respond to my phone calls. When I was finally able to contact him by phone and convince him to come meet with me, I explained to him what was happening; he had caught the fear disease from the other Afghan believers. I explained that he needed to resist that fear with everything in him by exercising extraordinary faith and trusting in Jesus for his protection and success in doing the Lord's work. After that conversation, along with much prayer from my prayer partners back home, Bashir made the decision to continue training with me.

Bashir trained with me most days for over three months. We discussed often how fear was our greatest enemy and any fear, however slight, had to be opposed, challenged, and overcome. I taught him to never give in to fear, to not even give it an inch of space in his heart or mind lest it continue to grow. I reminded him on an almost daily basis that by exercising extraordinary, crazy faith in Jesus, and by being bold in sharing His message of salvation with the lost, he would become like a magnet that attracted the attention of Jesus and His angels. Therefore, it was far safer to boldly share about Jesus than to hang back in fear.

Now that Bashir understood the bridge method, he would conduct the training of other Afghans. I had developed a guide to be given to Muslim seekers so they could look up the verses in their own Qur'an, and during their training they would receive that guide, along with a New Testament in Dari. It was not unusual for a Muslim to share the information we gave them with their family and friends, even before they had made the decision to repent and accept Jesus as Savior and Lord.

Chapter 25

An Attack Next Door and My Arrest

The workers at Werner's office usually left by 4:30 P.M. The local guy who lived in the room across the hall from me had an active social life, so most afternoons and evenings he was out with his friends, which left me alone in the building.

One evening I was doing some work in the office area when I heard some loud bangs. I thought it was someone banging on the gate, which would be unusual at that hour. Going out to check, I realized the sounds were gunshots from automatic weapons nearby. Curious, I went outside the gate to see what was going on and saw people running past me on both sides of the street—some were crying, obviously traumatized and scared. A young man came running by and I recognized him as a friend of the man who lived across the hall. He told me what he had seen.

He said he was walking on the sidewalk when he suddenly heard gunfire on the property across the side street from our building. It was a huge and impressive house owned by a very important local politician. When he looked up at the house, he could see people shooting, and a young girl fell off the balcony.

Many people were fleeing down the sidewalk past us while automatic gunfire continued in the background. A police car arrived on the street and the officers ordered us to go inside. We went up to my room and listened as the gunfire continued. Suddenly there was a loud explosion that shook the walls of my room. Though it sounded much closer, it was from the house that was being attacked. We waited for nearly an hour as we heard more gunfire and several more explosions. When the intervals between gunfire became longer, the young man decided to return home. He suggested I come along to get out of this dangerous area, but I declined. The shooting continued intermittently for the next 90 minutes. Then it became very quiet. The police cars left from the street in front of our gate, and it seemed the attack was over, so I went to bed.

About 30 minutes later I suddenly awoke to the sound of gunfire and explosions coming now from multiple directions. There was gunfire in the street right in front of my bedroom window. A couple bullets glanced off the metal gate below my window when I realized that I was in the middle of a firefight between the terrorists and the police. Apparently, the police cars had left the scene earlier because the terrorists had brought in reinforcements.

Around midnight there was still gunfighting in the streets, but I decided to go back to bed. There was a large picture window positioned at about knee height and at right angles to the street. It faced the length of the street where much of the fighting was happening. My bed was directly across the room from that window. As I lay down, it occurred to me that since the gunmen were shooting down the street, if a stray bullet went high and to the right, it could come right through the window, placing me directly in the line of fire.

Realizing my exposure, I decided to sleep on the floor below the window line, just to be on the safe side. I suddenly felt ridiculous and wondered why I had done that so automatically. I said aloud, "Lord, I assume angels can deflect bullets, right?" I reminded myself that nothing could harm me unless Jesus allowed it. I apologized to Jesus for showing fear and such a lack of faith as I left the floor and climbed back into my bed.

Sporadic gunfire and explosions on the street outside my room interrupted my sleep throughout the night. In the early morning one last explosion shook the building and rattled the windows. I found out later that it was the last of the attackers detonating his suicide bomb vest inside the house they had invaded.

After the last explosion, everything went eerily quiet. Later that day the media reported that one of the President's senior advisors, along with another politician, several bodyguards, and a policeman, had been killed in the attack by the terrorists. There was no mention of the drawn out fighting that had gone on in the streets. Given the lengthy street fighting, however, I suspected more people had been killed than the number being reported.

And Then My Arrest

The morning after the attack I went out to see the damage that had been done to the invaded house. I had my camera with me, and I took some photographs from the street. That turned out to be an unfortunate lack of judgement. As I was taking photographs a guy came up to me and tried to grab my camera. I didn't know who he was, so I held onto my camera as he tried to take it from me. When I realized he was there is an official capacity, I offered to delete the pictures and hand over the SD card. Evidently the man was a VIP within the secret police. I was immediately arrested and forced into a nearby police truck.

Driving to the police station in the back seat of the police truck gave me time to assess my situation. I quickly realized that I was in a bit of a pickle and possibly in far more trouble than just taking unauthorized photographs. I had a Dari New Testament MP3 player in my pocket and my Blackberry cell phone held emails describing what I was doing in Afghanistan. I was also carrying a USB with the training manuals in both English and Dari. Finding all these materials on me would undoubtedly lead the officials to my room, where I had over 50 Dari New Testaments and Bibles, over 100 Dari New Testament MP3 players, plus multiple printed copies of the training manuals. Having one Bible or MP3 in the Dari language may not have been a big problem. But the stockpile of materials I had in my room was a *huge* problem. There was no way I could casually explain my stockpile of evangelism materials.

Worse still, when I left the office Bashir was sitting at my desk. In my desk I had at least six Dari Bibles along with some MP3's and training manuals and other materials used to share the gospel. If the police searched the office, Bashir would be implicated too, and possibly the other Afghans in the office as well. I truly was not concerned about what would happen to me as I had been expecting much worse for a long time. But to find so many Dari Bibles and other materials in Bashir's proximity could have been a disaster for him. My priority was to protect Bashir and the other Afghan believers from the police. So, I prayed the Lord would do a miracle to protect these Afghans. As I usually do when I get into tough situations I told Jesus, "Lord, You have a real problem here. Yes, I got myself into this mess, but You sent me here and there's nothing I can do, so it's Your problem now."

At the police station I was taken to an interrogation room where the secret police captain and the officer who arrested me grilled me with questions. They demanded that I show them my passport. I was not carrying my passport, or any ID at all, which made them pretty upset. I never carried those things with me because if I had been robbed, they would be stolen. And if I was arrested or kidnapped, they would know who I am. They continued demanding my passport and I just kept repeating that I didn't have it with me. During the interrogation my Dari language skill was unusually and surprisingly good. I was able to explain myself properly and clearly, and I knew that Jesus was helping me, so I was calm and relaxed.

The police captain told me to empty all my pockets onto the small table in front of me. I did so and the officer sitting next to me began to examine each item very carefully. The most implicating things were the MP3 and the USB. I knew if they turned the MP3 on, or looked at the files on the USB, what they discovered would prompt them to search where I was staying.

I started to pray, "Lord I don't mind going to prison, but I always thought it would be for preaching the gospel, not for taking photographs. I don't want to be the cause of Bashir and the others being jailed, so please stop them from going to the office. Please blind their eyes and their understanding. Don't allow them to turn on the MP3, or to ask me what it is, or ask what is on the flash drive." I knew if they asked me what was on the MP3 and the USB that I was not going to lie, since I knew that Jesus would not want me to. I was silently and fervently praying while the officer went through everything on the table. He asked me several questions and then he picked up the MP3. As he picked it up I quickly prayed, "Jesus, please confuse his mind." He took the MP3 out of its plastic bag, looked it over and then turned to me. As he opened his mouth to ask me what it was, he suddenly looked confused. He shook his head, looked away, and put the MP3 back on the table. He next picked up the USB, taking the cap off and trying to stick it into the Blackberry. It seemed like he was about to ask me a question, but again, he looked confused and put it back on the table.

The police captain was telling me how bad it was for me to be taking pictures of the house. He kept saying that they will need to get my passport. He told me that he would put me in prison or cancel my visa and throw me out of the country. He said I was the enemy of the people. I said I was a friend to the people and that I was not the enemy, and I explained that I was in Afghanistan to help the people. This discussion went back and forth for quite some time. I had complete calm and peace, which I think was helping my situation.

The officer sitting next to me was still examining my belongings. Once again, he picked up the MP3 from the table and removed the battery cover and inspected it very carefully. I prayed, "Jesus please confuse him again and cause him to not turn it on or ask me about it." Again, he turned towards me and opened his mouth as if to speak. It was obvious that he was going to ask me what it was, but just as before he seemed to pause mid-thought, his face contorting into a look of abject confusion, and then he just stopped, turned away from me, and placed the MP3 back on the table.

The captain asked me to pass him my camera from the table, so I picked it up. As I was standing and passing the camera to him, I heard Jesus say to me, "Your turn now." I was a little confused by that, but as the captain put the camera on his desk and was examining it, it was made clear to me what I was supposed to do. I said to him, "It's a really nice camera, and it has a 4 gigabyte SD card, so you can take hundreds of pictures with it." I sounded like a camera salesman. He asked, "What should we do with the camera?" I said, "Considering how much trouble it has caused me, I don't want it anymore. I won't be taking any more pictures in Afghanistan." He asked again, "What should we do with it?" I said, "I will give it to you as a gift if I can leave right now." He said, "No, we still need your passport." I said, "Okay, I will get my passport, but the camera is mine, no gift. But if you let me leave here right now, with no passport, I will give you the camera as a gift." He replied, "No, we will need your passport for sure." He continued looking over the camera very carefully. I waited a few minutes, then I said, "This is your last chance; either you agree to take the camera as a gift and let me go right now, or I will keep the camera." At that he nodded his head and made a sweeping gesture with his hand. I quickly gathered all my stuff from the table. I was free.

What a miracle this was. They didn't come to the office and search and find all my materials. No harm came to Bashir or the other Afghans at the office. The police did not have any information on me, they didn't even know my name. Nor did they know where I lived, or what I did. All this meant the training in Afghanistan could continue. The result couldn't have worked out any better than it did. Once again, Jesus did the impossible.

Chapter 26

Fear Not!

Training Bashir was a great blessing from God. He quickly absorbed everything I was teaching, including my passion and love for Jesus and the Bible, as well as my faith and trust in Jesus. One day I would teach him something and the next day he would repeat it back to me. But he wasn't parroting my words. Instead, the Holy Spirit would instill the knowledge in his heart and mind as a revelation. It was comforting to know that Bashir would soon not need me at all, because he could so clearly hear the voice of Jesus and knew how to respond to the Holy Spirit. Soon Bashir was leading most of the training classes for the Afghans, teaching them how to teach others.

An important element of training the Afghan believers was inspiring them to not be fearful, to fear only God, and to trust Jesus and the Holy Spirit for protection. Yes, Afghanistan was an extremely dangerous place. But I explained that if they were bold in sharing the gospel with others, and they trusted Jesus, anything that happened to them would be only because Jesus allowed it. When I expressed those beliefs, it was not uncommon for one of them to say that God would not want the Afghan believers to be killed for their faith. I would counter that by explaining that ten of the twelve disciples who walked personally with Jesus were killed for their faith. I told them that being prepared to die for Jesus was a big part of faith and obedience to the Lord.

This counselling emphasized that it was necessary to have faith in Jesus to advance the gospel in Afghanistan in a bold manner, just as the first Christians had done after Jesus was resurrected. Jesus promised to never leave us or forsake us, and He had commanded that we should go into all the world and preach the gospel to every creature. But He also promised that we would suffer persecution for His name and the gospel, and that some would be killed. Muslims highly respect martyrs, and if Jesus allowed it, our deaths would make them more willing to listen to what other followers of Jesus had to say, creating an opportunity for many Muslims to receive eternal life.

The Afghan trainees were always very shocked when I said such things. Most of them had never been encouraged to share the gospel with their own families, let alone with strangers. Fortunately, the Bible provides many examples of extreme faith and boldness, and of the protections they could expect. I explained that Jesus and the angels are looking for and watching over those exercising extraordinary faith. Sharing the gospel in boldness is safer than not sharing the gospel at all. I recounted for them some of the many personal experiences where this held true in my walk with Jesus.

After listening intently to my viewpoints regarding fear and danger, they would often be quick to remind me that the protocol among many missionaries and their organizations was to not share the gospel with anyone they didn't know for at least three to seven years. But I could only respond that for us the Lord had reset the protocol from three to seven years to three to seven *minutes,* so that His goals for reaching Afghans with the gospel could be achieved before it was too late.

I must admit that once I see it in writing, I understand why they thought I was either crazy or had a death wish. And if Jesus is not faithful, and if His Word is not true, then I would be one of the most foolish and crazy people I know. But Jesus *is faithful*, and His Word *is true*. My willingness to take great risks and trust Him with my life may make me appear crazy, but it certainly doesn't make me foolish. They may be right about the crazy part, but they are wrong about me having a death wish. Rather, I have a life wish. How am I supposed to fear a death described in 2Corinthians 5:4 as "*mortality being swallowed up by life,*" and not long for that day when I get to leave this body of sin and pain behind and enter the presence of my Savior King Jesus? There is simply no downside to sharing the gospel boldly and trusting Jesus for all that happens as a result.

Chapter 27

What Happens When God Builds a Bridge

Only through the guidance of Jesus could I become so resolute about training the foreign missionaries in the bridge method. Not only so they could be far more effective, but so that they would speak encouragement to the Afghan believers and hopefully pass on the training to them. I was now led to have a formal training class for the missionaries at Werner's office.

I sent out emails to all the missionaries I knew informing them about the training class. I included my contact information and the time and location of the first meeting. I didn't receive much feedback or replies from the email, so was not expecting many of the missionaries to show up. But when the time for the first class came, the turnout was amazing.

The email did generate some interest and apparently the missionaries who encouraged my efforts put the word out. There were 14 attending the first training class. Clearly there was a hunger from the missionaries to share the gospel with the Afghans, along with an openness to learn new ways to share. Part of my training in the bridge method is to identify where the Lord is working and then join Him there. I realized this was key for the Afghan believers becoming bolder, by observing the boldness growing in these missionaries. Jesus was clearly doing a spirit-changing work in the hearts of these brothers and sisters.

At that first meeting I felt the need to speak out against the spirit of fear that was paralyzing many of the missionaries and the Afghan believers. Attacking this fear prompted much repentance from the missionaries for having given into the spirit of fear and infecting the Afghan believers with it. It was heart-warming and encouraging to see such open repentance and the enormous change in their hearts.

Following this initial meeting the missionaries used their excitement to encourage other missionaries. As a result, the second training class had more than 30 missionaries in attendance and the room was packed! There were missionaries from many different countries, both young and old.

I was praising Jesus silently while more missionaries entered the room. I almost fell out of my chair when I saw a man named Arthur enter. He was a Christian leader from Europe who had been serving in Afghanistan for several decades and he had a lot of influence with many of the other leaders in Afghanistan. I had previously learned that Arthur was one of the most outspoken of the Christian leaders against my work in Afghanistan. At first, I thought he might be there to collect evidence to prove to himself that I was inciting danger, and maybe that was originally his intention. But after the meeting he was extremely friendly and complimentary toward the bridge method training. He even said he would encourage an Afghan believer who worked for him to also take my training class. That breakthrough was exactly what I had been praying for. He later wrote an email encouraging me to continue conducting the training classes and asking for as many materials and resources as I could produce.

We had several more training classes and the enthusiasm continued. The people attending understood where my heart was. With all the information in the training manual, it meant they now had a step-by-step method for sharing the message of salvation with any Muslim they knew.

One older woman who had served Jesus with her husband in Afghanistan for decades told me it was the best method for reaching Muslims with the gospel she had ever seen. She came to every class. Another woman, a doctor, excitedly told me she had been serving in Afghanistan for nine years, and for the first time since her arrival she was now equipped to share the gospel with Muslims she knew and met.

A woman who had previously shushed me when I said the name of Jesus while conversing with her outside her home, for fear neighbors would overhear, attended the second meeting. After the class she asked if I would share the gospel with an Afghan man who worked for her. Bashir and I went to share the gospel with the young man, and ironically, we were outside in her yard where we could be overheard by her neighbors. Bashir did an excellent job sharing the gospel and the young man repented and accepted and received Jesus as Savior and Lord. It was always so awesome to see an Afghan leading another Afghan to saving faith in Jesus. God's plan was being fulfilled before my eyes.

The final night of training for the missionaries was astonishing. There was a spirit of faith present and an eagerness to share the gospel with Muslims that I had not previously witnessed in Afghanistan. The missionaries were abandoning deep seated prejudices about how to witness to Muslims and were embracing an approach that is much more loving, effective, and safe. I was in complete awe at what Jesus was doing. Jesus had done the impossible when He drew many of the missionaries to the training class, and He had even brought a couple of the Christian leaders as well. I knew that I was witnessing a great miracle from His hand.

After returning to the USA the encouragement and blessings continued. I learned that some from the group of missionaries were planning to continue meeting once a month to exchange experiences and encourage one another in using the bridge method. I was also receiving many positive emails from those who had taken the training class. For some it had completely altered their outlook on being in Afghanistan and allowed them for the first time to fulfill their callings to share the gospel with Afghans.

The missionaries were also passing on the bridge method training manual to others all over the world. I met a pastor later in the USA who had sent the training manual to a missionary his church had been supporting in Indonesia for many years. Several months later the pastor called me to tell me what happened after the missionary received the training manual. The missionary reported he had been in Indonesia for many years yet had never brought anyone to faith in Jesus. But after studying the training manual he visited a man whom he had been trying to reach with the gospel for years. Using what he learned in the training manual, the man not only was interested, but he immediately made the decision to repent and to accept and receive Jesus as his Savior and Lord. The missionary and the pastor were extremely thankful and excited at the difference it made to their ministries.

From my experiences serving in Afghanistan over an eight-year period, I learned that the entire country is a harvest field that is now over-ripe. The seeds for the harvest were planted by missionaries, faithful servants of Jesus who served sacrificially for many years. The seeds have been watered by other missionaries, many who are still there, and others who have gone there more recently. They have all served and loved the Afghans in the name of Jesus. They have given of their efforts and their resources. And some have even given their lives in faithful service to the Lord. Now it is harvest time.

It was about two weeks before I was to leave Afghanistan. I had just finished the final training class for the missionaries and went up to my room to relax after a very long and exhausting day. As I was sitting at my desk, Jesus began to speak to me; "Garry, you have accomplished everything I sent you here to do. Your work here is done."

I was initially shocked to hear that news. It had been a difficult journey for me to be working in Afghanistan for so long. With my health issues it was almost impossible at times. But His love and grace proved to be more than enough to keep me going, and I had grown to almost enjoy being so far out of my comfort zone. I had assumed that I would be coming back to Afghanistan many more times. I knew that I would miss the honor and privilege of being able to share the Good News about Jesus with people in Afghanistan who had never heard it before. And I would really miss the good friends I made—the Afghans and missionaries alike. But before departing Afghanistan for the last time, Jesus had yet one more incredible adventure for me to experience.

Chapter 28

Jesus Saves My Life

Increasingly I was being drawn to a mosque which I passed whenever leaving the property to catch a bus or taxi. This mosque was huge, housing not only the massive mosque, but also a school for kids of all ages, and a religious college where mullahs and other religious scholars were trained. The property and the street outside the compound were often a hubbub of activity. People of all ages were coming and going during the day, especially when students were starting and ending their classes.

I had been told that this mosque was the largest Shia Mosque in Kabul. Perhaps that was part of its draw because I felt Jesus was asking me to take an even greater risk on this trip. I felt He wanted to show me the limits on my work since I had developed a very determined heart to speak with more Muslim leaders about Jesus and the Bible.

During 2009 I met a couple of mullahs and shared the gospel with them, but they were part time mullahs rather than leaders over a large congregation. On this trip I had knocked on the doors of several mosques as I came across them, hoping to meet with the mullah, but each time was told that the mullah was not available to speak with me. So, I set my sights on trying to meet with the senior mullah of this particularly huge mosque. And one day I mustered up enough crazy faith courage to enter the property.

I walked through one of the main entrances of the compound which led to a guard station. I told the two guards that I wanted to see the senior mullah. After some phone calls and questioning,

I was asked to explain why I wanted a meeting with the mullah. I answered that I was a follower of Jesus and had been reading the Qur'an and wanted to ask the mullah some questions about the Qur'an. The senior mullah was not on the property at that time, so I was instructed to return on Sunday morning at 8:00 am. The guards assured me the mullah would be there at that time.

As directed, I arrived at the guard station promptly at 8:00 that Sunday and after a short wait was escorted into a private room. Not long after, the mullah came in with his entourage of five men. The mullah was a very tall man, well over six feet tall, with a large black turban on his head, and he towered high over my short frame. He was dressed in long black robes and wore shoes with high heels that added to his stature. It felt as if I was looking up at a giant.

We exchanged greetings and I was introduced to his security detail and assistants accompanying him. Before the meeting I was committed to maintaining my composure during the conversation. While I never get angry during conversations with Muslims, I am a very animated speaker and can become quite passionate, especially when speaking about the gospel. To not overtly offend the mullah, I was determined to listen respectfully and speak calmly.

The mullah asked me what I would like to discuss. I replied that I had been reading the Qur'an and found some interesting things in it that I wanted to discuss with him. First, I pointed to some of the positive things that the Qur'an said about Jesus, including the verse that identified Jesus as the straight path, and I brought up the fact that in the Qur'an Muslims are instructed to follow and obey Jesus. Then I referred to the fact that more than fifty times the Qur'an refers to the Bible, and it says repeatedly that the Bible is true and correct. I noted that the Qur'an instructs Muslims to read and obey the previous books, which we know are the books of the Bible. The mullah did not disagree with any of the points I brought up, and after some discussion on these topics I inquired why the Muslims I had met in Afghanistan did not read the Bible as the Qur'an instructed them to do. I added that when discussing this with Muslims, they would say that the mullahs and elders told them not to read the Bible and that the Qur'an had replaced the Bible. Asking the Mullah if it was true that the mullahs and elders were teaching such things, his reply was, "Of course we know that the Bible of today has been changed and corrupted."

Immediately the Holy Spirit took over. I was instantly filled with righteous indignation and my determination to control my emotions was totally lost. It was like something was forced up from my belly and out of my mouth and I literally roared "NO!" obviously shocking everyone in the room. But I continued passionately, "How can you say such a thing? You call yourself a religious leader of your people, and yet you dishonor and disrespect the Word of God by saying the Bible has been changed and corrupted. You must know that the Qur'an says that God is all powerful and that nobody can change His Word. And here you are saying that man has changed and corrupted the Bible, which even the Qur'an says is the true Word of God. That is blasphemy!"

Without intending to speak that way, I realized that my outburst would be considered contemptuous and rude, and felt that I was probably in big trouble. I glanced over at the other men in the room and their mouths were hanging open with a look of frozen fear. None of them uttered a word. The mullah was also shocked and stared at me with a look of disbelief, and even I was shocked by my response to his statement. It was safe to assume that nobody ever spoke to him like that, but he quickly regained his composure and announced, "I have a meeting to get to. Can you come back on Tuesday at one o'clock and we can resume our discussion? And please bring an Afghan friend with you to interpret for you." I didn't know why he was asking me to bring an interpreter since they all obviously understood what I was saying. But I agreed to return on Tuesday with an Afghan friend. I knew that I had seriously offended the mullah. He had a very prominent position and was clearly not used to someone challenging and insulting him as I had. I suspected that by inviting me back he almost certainly had something nefarious planned for me. Yet I still wanted to return to share the gospel with him and ask him to repent and accept and receive Jesus as Savior and Lord.

Returning to the office, I shared with Werner and the Afghan workers what had happened with the mullah. I asked the Afghans if one of them would accompany me on Tuesday. I didn't know what I would be walking into, so I didn't ask Bashir to come. I assumed that if I brought him there was no way he could resist sharing the gospel with the mullah. With the vision of what Jesus had planned for him in training others, I felt that I could not put him at that level of risk. I knew that since the other Afghan guys in the office would definitely not be sharing the gospel, they would not be at risk. After assurances that he would be introduced only as my interpreter who did not share my views, which was true, Abdul agreed to accompany me to the meeting.

Knowing full well what might happen to me, I did a lot of praying over the next two days, asking Jesus if it was His will for me to return to speak with the mullah. Receiving no clear direction from the Lord, I decided that having the opportunity to share the gospel with the senior Shia mullah in Afghanistan would be well worth any risk. It would also give me the opportunity to demonstrate what I had been preaching to the other believers, that if we obey Jesus' command to; *"Go into all the world and preach the gospel to every creature,"* we will attract the attention of Jesus and the angels by jumping straight into the lion's den without any fear in our hearts. I was completely convinced that in casting all caution to the wind and trusting in Jesus alone, He would decide my fate. He would either supernaturally protect me, or allow me to suffer persecution and/or martyrdom. Either way it was a win-win situation and there was absolutely no downside for me.

The mullah was not on the property on Tuesday at 1:00 when we arrived, but he had left word with the guards to call him. Once the mullah was on the phone, the guard handed the phone to

Abdul. The mullah said he had been away from the mosque for a meeting, but they were making their way through bad traffic and to please wait for them. He stressed that he really wanted to meet with us and that we should wait.

As we waited just outside the guard station, we heard a large explosion that came from the south not far away. It was loud enough that the students walking through the property were visibly shaken, and the guards were immediately on high alert. One of the guards came over to us and suggested that we should leave and come back another time. I replied we had a scheduled meeting with the mullah, and he was on his way, so we preferred to wait.

About ten minutes later there was a huge explosion coming from the west. It was so powerful that the windows in the buildings around us rattled. It sounded as if the explosion might have been on the mosque property. The students were now fleeing the property and running to the street in the opposite direction of the explosion. The two guards rushed over to us and told us to leave NOW! We left and headed back to the office.

Later in the afternoon I asked Abdul to call the mullah to reschedule our meeting. (I have hearing problems and it's very difficult for me to converse in a foreign language over the telephone). The mullah's response to the call was interesting: "You escaped, where did you go?" Abdul's face turned white as he told the mullah he would call him back while quickly hanging up the phone. Facing me, he confirmed the mullah had used those very words, "You escaped!"

Abdul was convinced a trap had been set for us with a plan to kidnap us or have us killed. He said there was no way he was ever going back there. I understood, but I asked him if he would call the mullah again and set up a time for me to meet with him. He thought I was crazy, and he told me so. But I needed his help to contact the mullah and didn't want any miscommunication over the phone with my language and hearing limitations.

The call to the mullah was attempted several times over the next few days, but the calls would never go through. That seemed strange as other calls worked just fine. Abdul gave up and said I was on my own now, so I tried calling myself. No matter how many times I dialed the mullah's number the call never connected, and I repeatedly got a message saying the network was busy. I had never experienced that before in Afghanistan. Since I was leaving Afghanistan soon, and I still felt compelled to share the gospel with the mullah, I decided to visit the mosque the upcoming Sunday morning like I had previously. I reasoned that if the senior Shia mullah in Kabul came to faith in Jesus, he could have an incredible influence on the entire country. I was determined to share the gospel with him. Wisely though, I also asked Jesus to stop me if the meeting was not in His will for me.

And Just Like That, Jesus Stops Me

I had brought with me a highly ornate and very expensive leather-bound New Testament in Arabic which I had purchased in the USA for such a time as this. I wanted to give it to the mullah knowing that he would appreciate the beauty of the book, and the fact that it was written in Arabic might prompt him to read it. On Saturday night I made sure I had everything ready for my meeting with him the next morning and went to bed early.

Immediately when I laid down on the bed, I saw a flashing light even though my eyes were closed. The flashing light was not coming from outside but was happening within my left eye. Upon getting out of bed, the flashing continued. I immediately emailed my wife and asked her to research what it could be. Her search brought up a disturbing explanation for the symptoms—a detached retina.

I called Werner to get advice from Hannelie since she is a doctor. I could not reach Werner, but I left a detailed message requesting help. They showed up at my door within thirty minutes. Although she lacked the instrumentation to absolutely confirm her diagnosis, Hannelie was convinced I was experiencing a detached retina. She advised me to have surgery within twenty-four hours to prevent loss of vision to the eye. Unfortunately, there were no eye doctors in Afghanistan who could perform the necessary surgery. Although flying could damage the eye further, I would have to fly to Dubai the next morning and have surgery performed there. I would have to stay in Dubai for at least three weeks until the eye sufficiently healed before I could fly home. So as much as I wanted to meet the mullah in the morning, I did not want to lose my eyesight. With no other option available I packed that night for a flight to Dubai in the morning.

On the flight I thought through my options. I did not want to stay in Dubai for three weeks while recovering, as I knew I would go stir crazy with nothing to do. I decided that since I was in the hands of Jesus, I would trust Him to protect my eye and I would fly home for surgery in Dallas. I felt peace about that decision.

As soon as we landed in Dubai, I talked my way onto a flight to Houston by citing the medical emergency. From Houston I would catch a flight to Dallas where surgery could be scheduled. As soon as the plane lifted off the ground, I felt the discomfort in my eye easing. Relief! No longer was there a flashing light in my eye nor was there any discomfort or pressure at all in my eye, and my eyesight normalized as well. I was amazed and astonished. I had been warned the eye would get worse with the flight due to the air pressure. I knew what was really happening, and I praised Jesus all the way home. I thought I would still need surgery to reattach the retina, but that Jesus was protecting my eye until it could be done. I was in great spirits for the rest of the flight.

The flight was uneventful, and the next morning I called an eye surgeon. The doctor, who happened to be Muslim, agreed to see me immediately due to the symptoms I described. Examining my eye, the doctor seemed astonished and asked, "Have you had recent surgery on this eye?" When I replied that I had not, he asked, "Have you *ever* had surgery on this eye?" Since my response was still no, he examined me further with a larger lens and a more powerful light. He mumbled some words I couldn't understand, then he asked me, "So, you got these symptoms three days ago, but you haven't had any surgery done on the eye since then?" "That's correct." I replied. "And you are sure that you have never had surgery on your eye in the past?" "No, I've never had any kind of eye surgery." "Well," he said hesitantly, "I'm not sure what exactly I am looking at. There is a lot of material floating around in your eye and it appears that at one point your retina was detached, but it looks like it was reattached. But the reattachment appears unusual and is unlike anything we would do in surgery. It's much finer than we can do. I'm not sure what I am looking at, but I can tell you that currently your retina is attached. Your eye looks good. It's all very strange."

I took the time to explain to him that I was not surprised. I explained what happened with my eye as soon as the plane took off from Dubai. I told him that I was certain Jesus had healed my eye and he looked at me in confused wonder. I think he just couldn't wrap his mind around what had happened. I was advised to return in two weeks for a recheck but was again told everything was in order with the retina!

As I mused over the doctor's report all the pieces began to come together. I was amazed at how Jesus was able to thwart the plans of the mullah. Jesus' complicated plan to protect me from serious danger, and most likely losing my life, was brilliant. Apparently, I had crossed the line that I had been looking for by insulting the senior Shia mullah in Kabul. Accusing him of blasphemy after he disrespected the Bible was clearly too much! In the last days that Jesus had me in Afghanistan, I finally found out where the line was, but Jesus. Jesus had saved my life so that I could continue to serve Him.

Coming home from Afghanistan with no further trips planned was unusual for me, and in many ways difficult. I had been so focused on my mission there, and it was a relief to have accomplished it. Yet, I missed the mission field. I missed relying on Jesus for every little thing. I missed the incredible number of divine appointments and doors miraculously opened, while other doors closed, also miraculously at times. I missed seeing Jesus move almost daily on my behalf in impossible situations. But I was also ready and willing to take a break and get some much-needed rest.

Chapter 29

Life After Afghanistan

I had no idea at the time if Jesus wanted me to retire from the mission field or if He had something else planned for me. Although I love to share the gospel with people, I truly am a home body and my health is quite poor, so going to the mission field means I am always out of my comfort zone.

I was only "on break" for a few months when I received a burden for Native Americans. Having spent my last three years of high school among many First Nation People in Canada, I could empathize with their struggles and challenges. It was no surprise to me when Jesus directed me to minister on the Pine Ridge Indian Reservation in South Dakota, my new mission field. I spent a large part of the next two years ministering there and meeting many wonderful people. I had some truly remarkable experiences and I saw souls saved and was able to encourage others in ministry. To this day I continue to be involved in assisting some of the native people as needs arise. After spending the better part of two years on the Reservation, Jesus directed me to leave Pine Ridge and He asked me to write a book about my life's journey. It has taken me a long time to finish writing this book and get it published, and I have learned a lot from the experience.

What's Next?

Jesus not only saved my soul, but He has saved my life many times. I have shared a few of those near-death experiences, and the attacks on my life have continued. In the past few years, I have experienced several health challenges that should have killed me. I had a massive heart attack in 2017 caused by a 100% blockage of the "widow maker" artery. It was more than four hours before I got to the hospital and into surgery, so my survival at that point is considered unusual. This was followed by an uncontrollable Crohn's flareup in late 2020 lasting more than three months and resulting in the removal of my entire colon. The surgeon was shocked that I hadn't already died considering the extensively damaged condition of my colon, as it literally fell into pieces in his hands. I told him I could explain in one word how I survived: His name is *Jesus*. That surgery was on New Year's Eve, thus ushering me into 2021 living a different kind of life. On July 4th of that same year, I suffered a second massive heart attack, which, because a cardiologist misdiagnosed the precursor symptoms a week earlier, continued for two days. Even the heart surgeon and cardiologists are amazed that I survived since that artery was also 100% blocked. While preparing me for surgery to place two stents in the blocked artery, my heart stopped. Because I have a "Do Not Resuscitate" order, the surgeon could not do anything to revive me. But it was not my time to go, and Jesus simply restarted my heart. I now sport four arterial stents.

Clearly Jesus was, and still is, keeping me alive for a reason. Through all these health issues, Jesus supernaturally preserved me so that I could continue to serve Him in reaching more souls with the gospel. While in the hospital I had multiple opportunities to share the gospel with the hospital workers. Everyone, nurses, doctors, technicians, cleaners, all heard about Jesus and his gift of salvation. I had a remarkably effective hospital ministry. It was awesome!

Since recovering from those dramatic health events, Jesus answered my prayers for connecting me with others locally who are willing to go out to share the gospel, by arranging a divine appointment with two wonderful brothers in Christ, Aaron and

John. These two brothers were saved about two years ago and they are both extremely obedient to Jesus' command to *"Go into all the world and preach the gospel..."* We have spent some wonderful times together sharing the gospel with strangers in our city. Because of their obedience to Jesus, these two men are being used in a mighty way, and their journey has only just begun!

Chapter 30

Eternally Grateful for the Gift of Crazy Faith

I have often wondered why Jesus allowed satan to do so many malicious and never-ending attacks on me throughout my life. And why He allowed me to endure so much physical and emotional pain. It seems so much of my life has been a continual physical and emotional battle. Yet I can see Jesus' wisdom in allowing these circumstances. I have certainly become much more compassionate to the struggles of others. Would my life have been as focused on sharing the gospel if the circumstances had been different and my life had been more comfortable? Would I have experienced and adopted a crazy kind of faith?

The things that have happened in my life extend far beyond me or my wishes. In the flesh I would have chosen a comfortable life, but Jesus is not seeking my comfort. He said in His Word that life for His followers would have troubles. He is seeking lost souls, and I have voluntarily surrendered my free will to His will, for the great blessing of being involved with Jesus reaching lost souls with the gospel. Of my own free will I gave Him permission to do anything or allow any circumstances in my life if it means even one more soul being saved from hell to join His glorious Kingdom. That is a prayer I have prayed many times. Since it aligns with His perfect will, Jesus has always honored and answered this prayer.

I am so glad that I know who Jesus is and have received the gift of salvation that He purchased for us on the cross. Just knowing that truth means I have no need whatsoever to fear death. I praise God for those in my family who have also been saved, my wife Janet, my sister Debbie, and my mom (who was saved at 75 years old). But I fear for my two brothers who have rejected God's free gift of salvation. I pray for them often, that their hearts will be open and God will grant them repentance so they may know the truth. I fear, too, for the billions of other people who have also rejected salvation. Watching people reject Jesus is like watching a boat sink and offering a lifeline to the drowning passengers, but they reject it. You long to help save them, but since they won't grab the lifeline and be saved, they perish without hope. My hope and prayer is that through the power of the gospel many more will repent and receive the precious gift of eternal life through Jesus Christ. May many who read this book be encouraged to seek out the lost to share the saving message of the gospel far and wide. And maybe a few will experience the privilege of developing an obedient, *crazy faith*.

Epilogue

I pray that this book has been an encouragement to you. I acknowledge that I am nothing special among men. I am not eloquent or charismatic in speaking, nor do I have a commanding presence. I have no title, special education or training, and I am without connections, recommendations, or acknowledgement from prominent people. My point in stating this is to merely show that if Jesus can use me to serve His purposes, He can use anybody. He can use you!

All that is required to be used by Jesus is a willingness to follow and obey Him. To simply do anything and everything that He asks you to do. A measure of crazy faith helps too. You will learn to have crazy faith as you exercise the little bit of faith that Jesus gives to each one of us when we are born again in His name. As you exercise that little bit of faith, Jesus will delight in it, and He will honor it by giving you more faith. Be diligent to exercise all the faith He gives you, and before you know it you will be living and walking in *crazy faith*. I can assure you there is no better place to be.

Serving Jesus and allowing Him to use me to reach lost souls with the saving message of the gospel has been an honor and a privilege like no other. I would not trade it for anything that the world could offer me. I pray that you will also discover that knowing and serving Jesus is the most fulfilling life that a man or woman could hope for.

Appendix

How to Share the Gospel

I know how difficult it is to share the gospel with people, whether they be friends or relatives, or complete strangers. The difficulty is not just with Muslims. When Jesus first called me to door-to-door and open-air evangelism, it was the most difficult thing I have ever done in my life. I had to drag myself to each encounter. Usually, I was hundreds or thousands of miles away from home, but sometimes even in the town I lived in. And He gave me zero anointing until I was right in front of an unsaved person opening my mouth to speak. Up until that point, there was no anointing, no gift of evangelism, only simple obedience to His command, *"Go into all the world and preach the gospel to every creature."* [Mark 16:15]. However, as soon as I was in front of an unbeliever and I opened my mouth with the intent to share the gospel, Jesus anointed me anew and gave me the words to speak.

Jesus is amazing! He doesn't ask a lot from us, which is why He was able to use even an introvert like me. Even though I don't have much to offer Him, still He says, *"As the Father has sent Me, I also send you."* [John 20:21]. I can tell you from experience that if we obey His commands, even though we bring nothing valuable to the table like in my case, He takes over and brings forth fruit that is sweet and lovely. That's because He is the One who does the impossible.

Below is one of the tools that I use to share the gospel. It is a copy of the sticker I have on the inside back cover of all my Bibles. First, I start a conversation with the unbeliever. When I sense that they feel comfortable speaking to me, I ask them if I can talk to them about Jesus and the Bible. Or I may just start by asking them, "Do you know what the Bible says about Jesus and Salvation?"

I start with the first Scripture, either reading it to them or asking them to read it out loud from the Bible. After each Scripture, I ask them if they understand what they just heard or read. If they say no, I ask questions to find out what they don't understand, and I discuss with them what it means. Then I go on to the next Scripture. If there is not enough time to go through all 14 Scriptures, then I will share those 9 Scriptures that are showing an Asterix (*).

Once I have shared and discussed the Scriptures, I will ask if they are ready to repent and turn from their sin and accept and receive Jesus as their Savior and Lord, and trust in Him alone for their salvation. If they say yes, I will lead them in a prayer for salvation. I read each sentence and ask them to repeat it after me. I remind them that they are praying to Jesus, not just repeating my words. If they say no, then I will share some of the other Scriptures I have listed below the prayer. If all else fails I will share 2Corintihians 5:18 - 6:2, and I encourage them to not receive the grace of God in vain, but to recognize their day of salvation. If they still say no, then I give them a tract that explains the gospel and has a prayer that they can pray when they are ready. There are many tracts available for purchase online or in Christian bookstores that explain the gospel and how to be saved.

I also want to mention the "Jesus at the Door" ministry (JesusAtTheDoor.com). They offer a tool and training that helps believers share the basic gospel easily and effectively. Since hearing about it I now use it often to share the gospel, and have found it to be the most effective tool I have ever seen for initially sharing the gospel with strangers. Once someone responds positively through using this tool, either immediately, or on our next encounter, I will go through the 14 scriptures below with the new believer so they will understand the gospel in more depth.

Salvation Scriptures

These are the 14 Scriptures I use to share the gospel.

Romans 1:16*
1 Cor. 15:3-4*
Romans 3:23*
Romans 6:23*
Romans 5:8
John 3:16-17 & 3:36
1 Timothy 1:15
John 3:3-6*
Mark 1:15*
John 1:12*
Ephesians 3:14-17*
Romans 10:9-10*
Ephesians 2:8
Revelation 3:20

Salvation Prayer

Jesus, I need You. I have sinned against You, and I am sorry. Please forgive all my sins and save me from the punishment of hell. I open the door of my heart to You. Please give me the gift of faith to believe in You, so I can trust You as my Savior. I choose to follow and obey You. I confess You now as my Savior and Lord. I believe that You died on the cross and rose from the dead so that I can have eternal life. Jesus, right now please fill me and baptize me with the Holy Spirit. In Your mighty name I pray this Jesus. Amen.

Other Important Salvation Scriptures

- John 14:6—*I am the way, the truth, and the life. No one comes to the Father except through Me.*
- Acts 4:12—*Nor is there salvation in any other, for there is no name under heaven given among men by which we must be saved.*
- Romans 2:4—*...the goodness of God leads you to repentance.*
- 2 Cor. 5:18-6:2—*...Behold, now is the accepted time; behold, now is the day of Salvation.*
- 1 Timothy 2:5—*For there is one God and one Mediator between God and men, the Man Christ Jesus.*

About the Author

Though raised an atheist, *Garry Bishop* always held a deep-seated emptiness in his heart. He spent a lot of time during his teen years in search of the meaning and purpose of life. Because of a rural lifestyle with little community support, and no religious education, his repeated attempts to find direction for his life and answers for his questions led only to discouragement and depression. Little did he know that Jesus was waiting for just the perfect moment—Garry's cry for help—to provide those answers Garry was seeking and to guide him to the path that would begin his journey.

Garry's journey has taken him to multiple mission fields throughout the world—Guatemala, Mexico, the Dominican Republic, the Amazonian jungle in Peru, India, Afghanistan, South Dakota—all for the purpose of sharing the gospel. And all at the unmistakable direction of Jesus. What an incredible, sometimes crazy, journey it has been.

Made in the USA
Coppell, TX
12 June 2026

80936197R00125